Jean Renoir:

Essays, Conversations, Reviews

Books by Penelope Gilliatt

ONE BY ONE
A STATE OF CHANGE
COME BACK IF IT DOESN'T GET BETTER
NOBODY'S BUSINESS
SUNDAY BLOODY SUNDAY
UNHOLY FOOLS

JEAN RENOIR:

Essays, Conversations, Reviews

by

PENELOPE GILLIATT

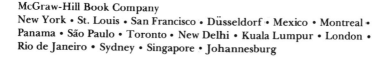

McGraw-Hill Book Company
New York • St. Louis • San Francisco • Düsseldorf • Mexico • Montreal •
Panama • São Paulo • Toronto • New Delhi • Kuala Lumpur • London •
Rio de Janeiro • Sydney • Singapore • Johannesburg

Library of Congress Catalog Card Number:

75-6905

0-07-023225-3

12345678910 MUBP 7654321069

Book design: *Hiag Akmakjian*
Cover design: *Robert L. Mitchell*

For Jean Renoir and Nolan

CONTENTS

Le Grand Monsieur de Deux Guerres, Libéré par Lui-même

JEAN RENOIR WAS BORN on September 15, 1894, in Paris. He was brought up there and at the old Renoir home, Les Colettes, in Cagnes, Provence. The great filmmaker has made and largely written 44 pictures, besides acting, doing an opera libretto, writing plays and a novel (*Les Cahiers du Capitaine Georges*), a biography of his father (*Renoir, My Father*) and a typically simple late biography of himself (*My Life and My Films*).

The genius of this most dear man, who takes part in the world with the wisdom, sense, and humor that reigns in his films, lies perhaps in his gift of intense concentration. His power of focus on the topic at hand is total. Of hobbies, for instance, he once said to me in Paris, "They are very charming, but if you are at work they are like physical training or gardening or brushing the teeth. One does the merest necessary when one is working, don't you think? If I worry about two things together I die in a week." On the other hand, there is the very opposite of ferocity in his absorption. He adores any arrangement of life, work, talk, sociability that has a just sense of balance. He said, again in Paris, "I spend my time reestablishing balance in a film but I have never had the idea that it should be established simply by means of elements in the plot. One can do it with an object on a table, with a color if it is a color film, with a sentence which means nothing at all but which has less weight or more weight than the sentence before it."

Renoir's friendship and conviviality first came into my
life through revivals of his early films and premières of his
later ones that I saw in London as a child, and then when I
began to go often to the Paris Cinémathèque and to the
National Film Theatre by the Thames to write about them:
always, I hope, in his sense of an "amateur" (Renoir sheers
away from "professionalism" as he defines it). His presence,
which cheers any day even now that he is ill in Los Angeles
and unable to travel, was something that I first encountered
when I was in Paris and writing a profile of him for *The New
Yorker*. This book is by no means a comprehensive book
about his films, although I have seen them many times. Nor
is it distantly analytic: his work forbids distance, since it
invites you into his company, like great music or Chekhov.
His work is eloquent enough to talk for itself, and so is he. I
hoped more to transcribe some of the taste and purity of his
conversation, and the mood and technique of the movies
that I particularly love. As to the lack of analysis proper,
I can only think of something Renoir once said to me on the
subject, with his usual absence of asperity: "There is a certain type of person who wonders if it is the eggs on the
muffin that make eggs Benedict."

What a man this is. What a span of work. Think of *La
Chienne*, his first true sound movie after the tests he made in
directing *On Purge Bébé*, with Michel Simon as a middleaged
Sunday painter innocently in love with a whore and a bitch.
Apart from its technical originality, which is still as striking
and necessary as true originality always is, the news-clipping
story is raised into something poetic, just as moments are in
his much later *Le Déjeuner sur l'Herbe*, where a film that could
be a mere satiric idyll of modernity becomes an idyll of the
Freezer Age. Like his great father, he also has the Impres-
sionists' love of the physical. When he photographs a pillow

that has just had someone lying on it, the shot has the insight and beauty of a Bonnard painting of a girl in a bath.

Somebody once wisely said that it is very easy to make art of evil but very hard to make art of good and evil. Renoir does it. He sees everyone, good and bad, with a mixture of sweetness and irony that some wrong-headed people have called amoral. Renoir is not disingenuous. No one who has been such an innovator could be. The bans and butcherings of his two prescient anti-Fascist masterpieces—*La Grande Illusion* and *La Règle du Jeu*—prove that all too well. Perhaps his born pacifism and his loathing of all divisions between people make him seem misleadingly mild now to a few arid members of the politically engaged. But just before the Second World War, when he was making *La Grande Illusion*, the antiwar nature of the film and its affectionate respect for the German commandant played by Erich von Stroheim were strongly unpopular attitudes in France. Renoir said in 1938, in an interview in *The New York Times* of October 23, that Hitler "in no way modifies my opinion of the Germans." He described the film to me as a "reenacted documentary, like *La Règle du Jeu*," and went on to say, "They are documentaries on the condition of society at a given moment. I made *La Grande Illusion* because I was a pacifist, I suppose. And am. At the time, the usual idea of a pacifist was of a coward with long hair yelling from a soapbox and getting hysterical at the sight of a uniform. So I made a pacifist film that is full of admiration for uniforms and escapes. The idea came to me in the thirties when an old friend of mine, named Pinsard, turned up in command of some nearby airfield when I was shooting a scene—for another film—that was driving me mad. This old friend had saved my life in 1915. A German flew so near to us that I could see his impressive whiskers."

La Grande Illusion was being shown in Vienna the day
the Nazis entered the city. It was stopped in mid-reel. The
history gives Renoir a certain amount of satisfaction. "We
had wanted to make the film for three years but no one
would put up the money," he said. "French, Italian, Ameri-
can, British producers saw nothing in the project. They
wanted a villain. They said the German to be played by von
Stroheim was not sufficiently a villain. I said the villain was
the war. 'The public won't understand that,' they said. Well,
finally a group of businessmen risked forty thousand dol-
lars, and at the end of the first year I believe the profit was
ten times the investment. You know, years and years before
that, in his *Foolish Wives*, von Stroheim pointed out something to me that I hadn't known at all. I saw that film twelve
times. It changed things. Something very simple I hadn't
known—only that a Frenchman who drinks red wine, and
eats Brie, with Paris roofs in front of him, can't do anything
worthwhile except by drawing on the tradition of people
who have lived like him. After *Foolish Wives* I began to look. I
mean, the movements of a woman washing her hair that we
might see through this window, or of that man with the
broom—I found that they were terrifically valuable plasti-
cally."

The prologue of *La Grande Illusion* happens in a bar
near the French Front where Lieutenant Maréchal (Jean
Gabin), a former mechanic, is asked to escort a smooth man
with a monocle, called Captain de Boïeldieu (Pierre Fresnay), on a mission behind enemy lines. The plane is shot
down by von Rauffenstein, played by von Stroheim, whom
Hollywood had dismissed as a wild-eyed esthete. Like de
Boïeldieu, he is an aristocrat and a career officer: he invites
the two Frenchmen to luncheon. Their prison camp room-

mates include a schoolteacher, a surveyor, an actor guilty of terrible puns, and a garment maker called Rosenthal (the great, delicate-gestured Marcel Dalio). There is no sense of class here. Everyone is hellbent on digging the escape tunnel that has already been started. There is a talent show: the effort of the prisoners to evoke the women they miss by putting on women's clothing is pathetic, though never sentimental and often funny. It is typical of Renoir's sense of absurd, bitter, passing catastrophe that, just as the tunnel is finished, the prisoners are moved on and replaced by Englishmen who speak not a word of French and can therefore make no use of the tunnel.

With a series of quick dissolves showing repeated attempts to escape—no one is more succinct about narrative than Renoir is, just as no one spends more time on irresistible irrelevancies—we see that Maréchal and Boïeldieu are now being hauled off to a disciplinary camp in a castle-fortress for their pains. They are greeted cordially by their enemy: von Rauffenstein again, stiff-backed from chin to waist in a leather corset that has to be worn because of a war wound. He is delighted to remeet de Boïeldieu, though he regards Maréchal as a rather unfortunate product of the French Revolution. De Boïeldieu is alone in realizing that his noble class is doomed. Rosenthal, Maréchal, and de Boïeldieu plan yet another escape by a plaited length of cloth. The escape is to be covered up by de Boïeldieu tootling a French folk-song from the ramparts. Von Rauffenstein, stricken that he should have to do his duty by killing his ally in caste, shoots him in the stomach. Maréchal and Rosenthal, beginning to quarrel, sprint for Switzerland on foot, Rosenthal with a sprained ankle. They take refuge in a farm where Maréchal falls hopelessly in love with a German:

again, Renoir's view of frontiers. They have to leave, though. Struggling on in the snow, they are spied by a German soldier. He starts to shoot. "Forget it," says a comrade, "they're in Switzerland."

The film swiftly states Renoir's view of a man's life as a state of being rather than an undertaking. It also perfectly expresses his view of the nonsensicality of divisions between people. No wonder Goebbels banned the film—remember that it was made in 1937, obeying Renoir's unfailing, urgent sense of malaise, a signal that he believes artists have to follow even if it means being dangerously in the lead ("In running faster than the others, the artist fulfils a function," he said to me)—and that the Nazi head of propaganda put pressure on Mussolini to prevent its being given a prize at the Venice Film Festival. Though the film is about the First World War, the ideas in it were to be perilously appropriate to the next. Wars, it says, are run for dictators and ideologists safely at their desks, an idea Renoir was to repeat in *Le Caporal Épinglé*. They will never be conducted in the interests of the men who fight them. The flag here is a remote symbol, and military honor is vapid; it is the fineness of grain shared by an aristocratic Frenchman, an aristocratic German, and a Jewish garment maker, not any empty idea of courage or belief in boundaries, that unites the characters. Renoir was to suffer for his warning of the sickness perturbing his contemporaries. The film was banned and the negative seized by the Germans (it was found much later by the Americans in Munich). A 1946 reissue was criticized for being kind to the Germans and for anti-Semitism, which is entirely to miss the spirit of this great tribute to tolerance. Like Luther, Renoir says politically, "Here I stand." For instance, he made *This Land Is Mine* during the war, in exile

in Hollywood, as a retort to the prevailing idea in America
that the European resistance movement was a legend and
that everyone in an occupied country was a collaborationist.

But, he said recently, "I believe now I see a state of
benevolence, of well-wishing. If I am wrong, people can
always laugh at me. I take that risk." About what he spoke of
as "the Czech affair," with sorrow, when the Russian tanks
had rolled in, he said, "It happened perhaps to save this
wild world, the miniskirts, the crazy singing in London, the
marijuana. I am trying to understand the Russians and what
is behind them in spite of themselves." His habit is to take in
the whole spectacle of paraphernalia and then to sort out the
essentials, just as he does in a minor way when he is working
on a set. He said, "I leave the propman to do what he wants,
but I ask him to do too much and then I take out almost
everything. I find it handy to have the choice. To crowd the
set and then to empty it." Everything interests him. In Paris,
watching a newsreel with me once, he was touched and
tenderly amused by a sequence showing the back view of a
plump Olympic girl solemnly running with a torch. "I am
against great themes and great subjects," said this maker of
two of the world's greatest films. "To me, a theme is exactly
like a landscape for a painter. It is just an excuse. You can't
film an idea. The camera is an instrument for recording
physical impact." The impact, for him, can lie in very small
details. In La Chienne, it lies in a small girl practicing her piano
on the far side of one of his favorite courtyards, in the sound
of a couple quarrelling somewhere, in the burble of a lady
talking. The impact is one of great weight, for the observation
is dense and exact. "I had a good friend who owned a theater
in Biarritz," he told me. "A very interesting man. A Russian
who had been a sailor in the Turkish navy. He could put a

coin somewhere, swing a blacksmith's hammer and stop exactly half an inch from the coin. With such a man you can be
confident." The words might have been said to commemo-
rate the confidence one feels about Renoir himself, just as *La
Grande Illusion* is an unwitting tribute to the nobility of his own
heart.

LONDON, NEW YORK, 1974

Le Meneur de Jeu

"LOOK AT THIS," SAID JEAN RENOIR in his Paris apartment, bending over an art book. "It is the Annunciation to the Virgin Mary, and the angel is just shaking hands. It is an interesting way to tell someone she is pregnant." He had been speaking French, but now he switched to English and repeated the last sentence, with characteristic absorption, substituting for "interesting" the word "funny," which he pronounces "fonny." The ideas of what is comic and what is interesting truly overlap for him. He looked out of the window and said that the roofs of Paris houses go at angles that always remind him of theater wings. A child was playing somewhere below in this offstage life, and a wife was shouting while her husband strolled away from her, pulling on his cap at a nonlistening slant and then putting his hands in his pockets. "The first films I made were very rotten," Renoir said. "Then I started to make a sort of study of French gesture, and maybe they improved, with the help of my accomplices." The sight of his own gestures as he was talking made me remember one of those fugitive shots which can break through his films so piercingly—a shot in his 1939 picture *La Règle du Jeu* of the plump character played by Renoir himself, the fortunate, poignant stooge, who has just idly let loose the fact that he would have loved to be a conductor. In a shot late at night, on the terrace steps of a grand country house, he can be seen for a second from the back in an image of the clown sobered, conducting the

invisible house party inside to the beat of some imagined
musical triumph. His big shoulders droop like the withers of
a black pig rooting in the dark. Recently, after I had spent
some time with Renoir, it struck me that the character
perhaps embodies a little of the way he thinks of himself,
and that this great, great master of the cinema, who has an
amplitude of spirit beyond our thanks, actually sees himself
as a buffoon.

   Renoir walks with a limp bequeathed by a wound from
the First World War. He has a blanched, large face, very
attentive, which turns pink as if he were in bracing air when
he is interested or having a good time. At the beginning of
the 1914 war, he was twenty. Nothing in our benighted
century seems to have undercut his sense that life is sweet.
He makes films full of feeling for picnics, cafés, rivers,
barges, friends, tramps, daily noises from the other side of a
courtyard. It is singular and moving that a man whose talent
imparts such idyllic congeniality should also have such a tart
and sophisticated understanding of caste. In his 1935 film
Le Crime de Monsieur Lange, for instance, the hero's world of
the badly off and hungrily gregarious is pitted against a boss
class of steely, swindling fops. The heroic Lange, who mur-
ders with our sympathy, is a young man who writes thrillers
in the time left over from a dull job in a printing plant.
Renoir's murderers are always strange to crime: an un-
happy clerk, a down-at-heel, derided lover, a gamekeeper—people near the bottom of the heap who take desperate action because they have been driven beyond their
limits. The limits usually have to do with what a man will take
in punishment to his dignity and his seriousness about how
to live, and his gestures state everything. There is the es-
sence of ache and hesitancy in Dalio's double turn, near the

end of *La Grande Illusion,* at the door of a woman who has
sheltered him while he was on the run from a prisoner-of-
war camp and whom he cannot quite declare his feelings for.
Renoir's own way of standing reminded me sometimes of a
shot of Michel Simon in *La Chienne,* his big head bent in
watch over a murdered woman. The tonic passion and
lightness of the dissolving shot would be recognizable as
Renoir's in a thousand miles of film. So would a special kind
of cheerful misrule that sometimes runs amok in a scene,
like the time his tramp Boudu, in *Boudu Sauvé des Eaux,*
lustily wrecks a room in the process of merely cleaning his
boots, carousing around the world with an abstracted seren-
ity in the midst of riot.

When Renoir is in France—he spends a lot of time in
America, at a house he and his wife, Dido, have in Beverly
Hills—he lives in an apartment close to the Place Pigalle, in a
rue privée with a black iron gate that is guarded, not very
vigilantly, by a caretaker. The little curved street inside is
lined with plane trees, and moss grows through cracks in the
pavement. There are elegant iron lampstands, and gray
shutters on the beautiful, run-down old houses. His apartment is on the second floor of a house with ivy spilling over
the front door. The stairwell is painted in a peeling burnt
sienna with a turquoise design. It is all very dilapidated and
very nice. "I think it's better when things aren't brand-new,"
Renoir said. "It's less tiring for the eyes." He sometimes
speaks of the apartment as if it were an obstreperous old
friend with long-familiar attributes, many of them a bit
grating but all indispensable. "I like the proportions," he
said one day, looking around at the place. "It's not entirely
convenient. When it rains, it rains in here." He showed me
drip trails at various points, accusingly. "But I like the pro-

portions. If you want to make me happy, you should feel absolutely at home."

In the drawing room, where he works, there is an old-fashioned telephone, paintings by child relatives, comfortable armchairs with springs gone haywire, ancient white-and-gray plasterwork on the walls, records of Mozart and Vivaldi and Offenbach. During the days we spent together talking, Renoir usually wore a tweed jacket and old leather moccasins—with a tweed cap when we went out—and he always had a pen clipped in his jacket pocket. We seemed to spend a lot of time in the kitchen. It has two tall windows, and between them a splendid freehand drawing in brown paint of a window with curtains looped back and a bowl on the sill. He did it himself. He said, "A mirror fell down and broke, and it left a patch, so I put up that piece of paper." I said that it wasn't a piece of paper: that it was a drawing, and looked rather like a Matisse. This so embarrassed him that I had to say quickly, "Matisse on an off day, with a headache." The drawing made a third window to look through, so to speak, when we were having lunch opposite it every day at his scrubbed kitchen table. Renoir's doctor recently gave him a choice of whiskey or wine, and he chose wine. We drank rather a lot of it, and cooked gigot. I mentioned Céline at one point, and he lowered his head and looked pleased. "Greater than Camus," he said. "He was entirely hidden for twenty years. He was not the fashion." Renoir was genuinely unable to think it right that I should have come all the way from New York to see him, and in the end I had to put it as if I were using him as a way station on a journey to my house in England. "I rather hate airplanes," he said. "We should be able to part the Atlantic like the Red Sea and drive across it in a bus. I'm fond of buses." We swapped bus stories.

We caught ourselves in a mirror one day as we were coming into the apartment, talking mostly about actors, whom he distinguishes from stars as though a star were to be removed from the matter with a long-handled pair of tongs. He made a face at our reflections and said, "To be a star and play yourself all the time—a beautiful doll imitating yourself . . ." Ingratiation is one of the few flaws that really seem to scrape on his nerves. He picks up any hint of it fast. He once remarked to a filmmaker whom we both know that there is something that bothers him in Chaplin's films, which in general he admires. He called it "an anxiety to displease nobody." Though Renoir's own films seem expansively charitable, they are altogether uncompromising. "I believe in the Tower of Babel, I suppose," said Renoir. "Not in the story, exactly, but in the meaning. The tendency of human beings to come together. My first attempts at filmmaking probably didn't find this point. But one gets into practice. When things go badly on a film, I think I will go and raise dogs, and then the crisis blows over. At one moment I feel that a story is terrible and at the next that it's wonderful, and in rare flashes of lucidity I feel that it's neither good nor bad. And so, indeed, quite like everything else. I am very much in favor of intelligence, but when you are at work on a film or a story or a painting I think you have to go on instinct. In *La Règle du Jeu*, for instance, I knew only very roughly where I was going. I knew mostly the ailment of the time we were living in. That isn't to say that I had any notion of how to show evil in the film. But perhaps the pure terror of the danger around us gave me a compass. The compass of disquiet. You know, there is a sense in which artists have to be sorcerers twenty years ahead of their period. I don't mean that they are wiser than anyone else

—only that they have more time. And, well, though it is
much harder for an artist to do this in the cinema, because
the cinema insists on being an industry twenty years behind
the public, it can sometimes be done."

He turned out to be thinking now of many young film-
makers whom he admires, and to have left altogether the
topics of his own pictures and of his own shocking and
lifelong difficulties in raising money. At this moment, in
1968, he has virtually had to give up the prospect of making a
movie from a very funny script, written by him, which Jeanne
Moreau wants to play in. No financing can be found for it.
The situation seems commercially unintelligent. It is also an
offense, as if Mozart were to be deprived of music
paper. A short while ago, another script—a comedy about
revolt, which Simone Signoret wanted to do—similarly fell
through. In the meantime, Renoir remains not at all bilious
and works on other things. He is writing his second novel
—his first was called *Les Cahiers du Capitaine Georges*, and was
published in 1966—and directing a series of sketches, also
by him, for French and Italian television. He always declines
to fuss. I had the impression that he doesn't like weightiness
of any sort. In 1938, when he was abused by some people for
making a film of *La Bête Humaine* that wasn't slavishly true to
Zola, he stoutly said that he hadn't particularly wanted to
serve Zola, he'd wanted to play trains. "You have to remain
an amateur," he said to me one day about directing. "The
big problem is not to stop at being a voyeur. Not to look on at
people's predicaments as if you were a tourist on a balcony.
You have to take part. With any luck, this saves you from
being a professional. You know, there are a thousand ways
of being a creator. One can grow apples or discover a planet.
What makes it easier is that one isn't alone. One doesn't

change or evolve alone. However great the distance between them, civilizations move a little toward one another. And the worlds we know, the directions to which interest bends us in our knowledge or our affection, incline to be one in the same way."

A French television unit came one day to direct Renoir in part of the shooting for a long program about him and his father, the painter Auguste Renoir. He needed a companion for a walking scene in Montmartre, and I was the obvious person, although I told him that the only acting I had ever done had been on account of having red hair.

"Lady Macbeth," he said.

"Yes," I said.

He told me what it had been like at school for him because he had had red hair, as his father painted him in the famous childhood portrait. "And who else did they make of you?" he asked, stroking his head unconsciously. "The Pre-Raphaelites?"

"Agave in *The Bacchae*," I said. "For the same reason."

The French sound man said politely, after a long time, that he was getting only a moan from me on his earphones, and could I talk more loudly.

"Her diction in English is excellent," said Renoir.

"Now a new setup," the TV director said, after another long time.

"Which side do you prefer?" Renoir asked me.

I said that the next part might go better from the other side, because of my nose. Renoir took me by the shoulders and had a look at me.

"A girl ran into me in a corridor at school and bent it," I said.

"It's true," he said, nicely, and put me on his other side, and we moved around a lamppost. He held my wrist, perhaps to help himself travel a slope, and then slipped his hand up to my elbow to support me through the prospect of having a seven-word line to say, while he improvised a monologue of incomparable invention and warmth.

Some time later, I asked him about an actor I liked very much in *Monsieur Lange*. Renoir beamed, and said something incidental about his own way of working. "I'm pleased you pick him out. He was excellent, exciting, subdued. However—not that it mattered—it happened that he couldn't remember his lines easily. So the thing was to give him a situation where he had to say what he had to say. Where he couldn't say anything else."

And the same day—"He is the most French director," said the actress Sylvia Bataille, who worked with him on the 1936 film *Une Partie de Campagne* and on *Monsieur Lange*. "The most cultured. He has a sense of history like no one else's. He was the precursor of everything in French cinema now. You know, when he is directing you, he has a trick. Well, not a trick, because that sounds like something deliberate. A way of doing it—a habit, the result of his nature. He will say, 'That's very good, but don't you think it's perhaps a bit boring to do the next take exactly the same way?' He will never say that the next take is to be totally different because in the first one you were terrible. I think the reason he is a great director is that he knows all there is to know of the resolves that people keep to themselves. He knows the human reaction to anything. I'm not very good, but he made me magnificent."

There exists an affectionate French documentary of Renoir directing some actors. He listens to them as if through a stethoscope. Then he may talk of other times, the times of "Monsieur" Shakespeare, "Monsieur" Molière—speaking without sarcasm. Again and again he says, *"Trop d'expression."* He tries to get a highly charged actress to speak "like a telephone operator." There is a big moment, and he tells her not to be sweet. *"Soyons pas mignons."* It is always "us." *"Soyons secs."*

"If actors look for feeling at the beginning of a reading, the chances are it will be a cliché," he said to me. "When they learn the lines alone or when we learn them together—the second being the better—in either case I beg them to read as if they were reading the telephone directory. What we do is to read a few lines that can help the actors to find the part. Pick a few lines that are symptomatic. Now, what happens then is that, in spite of himself, the actor begins to find a little sparkle, provided he forbids it. Whereas if you begin to play with feeling, it will always be a generality. For instance, suppose an actress playing a mother has to speak of 'my son' when he is dead. For most actresses, it is the devil's job for this not to be a cliché if they begin with the sadness of it. And if you start with an idea of how to say it, then it is very difficult to remove it. You should start with the lines quite bare. You see, even in our day everyone is different from her neighbor, or his. We must help an actress to find a 'my son' that will be hers and only hers."

This strong feeling that people are different is obviously part of Renoir's great gift for friendship. I said something about disbelieving and fearing the cool comfort that everyone is replaceable and no one indispensable. He said securely, *"Everyone* is indispensable." We talked about Brecht, whom he was very fond of. They had fun together, loping along the streets by the Seine with some friends, in a

gang. "He was a very modest man, you know," Renoir said.
"Well, perhaps he was, like many modest men, proud inside.
He was a child. It's not so easy to remain a child. And he was
also sarcastic, which people never understand. He was
romantic but also sharp, and sharp people are not well
understood. We had many adventures. We wanted to make
films. I remember once we went for money to Berlin, to the
king of German cinema. We suggested a subject. He said no.
He said, 'You don't belong to the movies.' You see, he was
right. On the way home, Brecht said, 'Look, Jean, don't let's
make movies. We should call what we want to do something
else. Let's call it *pilm*.'"

When we were back in Renoir's living room after the
television shooting, he said to me, "In directing, I don't
follow a script very closely. And I think it works best to
choose a camera angle only after the actors have rehearsed.
I suppose that between my way of working and the one of
following a script closely there is possibly the same difference as between Indian music and Western music since the
tempered scale. In Indian music, there is a general melody,
and this general melody is ancient and must be held to, and
then there is also a general note played on a particular
instrument, and this note is repeated all the time and keeps
the other instruments up to pitch. And so there is a melody
and a pitch, and the musicians are free to move around these
fixed points. I think it is a magnificent method, and I try to
imitate it with actors and filmmaking, up to a point.",

We drifted into talking about Stanislavsky. Renoir said
that he had learned endlessly from Stanislavsky but that
Stanislavsky had "a big problem." He explained, "Often the
Moscow Arts Theatre had to speak in front of an audience
that didn't know Russian at all—or, if so, not good Russian.

It forced the company to make too many clear signals. To shout inner things, so to speak."

We sat in the drawing room on another day. "Excuse me," said Renoir. "My maid is here today and I want to know how she feels. She has a bad eye." He went out and stood talking with her, his head hanging down as he listened, like a fisherman's watching a river. She was insisting that she was all right and could work, making gestures with a dustpan: a short, alert woman, one eye covered with a patch of bright-pink sticking plaster. They stood there for a time, visible through two doorways and faintly audible, like people photographed in the unemphatic style of his films.

"She won't go home," said Renoir, coming back into the room. "She's very strong. She doesn't look it. She's built like a French soldier. Frederick the Great was amazed by how small we were. Just before a battle, he said, 'How can they fight?' " Renoir limped around and got some wine and said, "We lost, I believe." And then he sat down again and went on watching the woman for a while through the doorways. I looked at a photograph pinned up over his desk. It showed a cluster of men in cloth caps sitting on the ground and laughing. The scene looked rather like a factory picnic, but not quite. Renoir said that the picture was by his friend Henri Cartier-Bresson and that the men were convicts. "When their sentences were over, they didn't want to leave the labor camp, so they just stayed. They had their friends, et cetera, et cetera. And also, you see"—he spoke seriously—"I think they'd come to like the work."

We talked about a London prison where I had once lectured and shown *La Règle du Jeu*. He asked a lot of questions, often using the words "interesting" and "interested," which sprinkle his talk, like "et cetera." "I quite enjoy lecturing when I'm doing it," he said. "Not so much when it's over. Doing it is generally the only thing, isn't it? One sees that even with banking, which God knows is a stupid occupation. But when a banker is actually making the money he thinks he needs to retire with, then he is happy, and with luck the retirement never arrives. I suppose I really believe work and life are one, as the Hindus do. When I'm making a film, for instance, I don't know where the divisions are in the job. When I'm writing, I'm cutting the film in my head. And when I'm cutting I'm doing more of the screenplay. You understand, this isn't to say that there aren't terrible days before we start, when nothing is possible." He paused, then went on, "But Hollywood, because it has this genius for departments, has found the perfect way to make pictures that have no sense. A producer has a wonderful screenplay, by wonderful authors—plural—and he puts wonderful actors in it, and then he hires a wonderful director, who says 'That's a little slow,' or 'Please be more warm.' And so—well, it is most efficient, and what it reminds me of is a perfect express train racing along perfect steel tracks without having any idea that one of its compartments contains a beautiful girl leaning against beautiful red plush with a most interesting story to tell. A lot of people who are quite sincerely critical of Hollywood say that the trouble is that the people there worship money, but I believe them to be worshipping something much worse, and that is the ideal of physical perfection. They double-check the sound, so that you get perfect sound, which is good. Then they double-check the lighting, so that you get perfect lighting, which is also fairly good. But they also double-check the director's idea, which is not so good. It brings us straight to another god—or perhaps I should say devil—that is very dangerous in the movies, and that is the fear that the public won't understand. This fear of 'I don't understand' is terrible. I don't see how you can ever understand something you love. You would not say that you understood a woman you love. You feel her and like her. It has to do with contact. Something many people ignore is that there is no such thing as interesting work without the contact of the public—the collaboration, perhaps. When you are listening to great music, what you are really doing is enjoying a good conversation with a great man, and this is bound to be fascinating. We watch a film to know the filmmaker. It's his company we're after, not his skill. And in the case of the physically perfect—the perfectly intelligible—the public has nothing to add and there is no collaboration. Now I am going to be very trite and say that it is easier to make a silent film than a talkie, because there is something missing. In the talkies, therefore, we have to reproduce this missing something in another way. We have to ask the actors not to be like an open book. To keep some inner feeling, some secret."

Renoir's feeling for ambiguity is powerful. He clings to doubt as if it were a raft. I told him about a playwright friend of mine called N. F. Simpson, the author of *One-Way Pendulum* and *A Resounding Tinkle*: wonderfully funny plays that some humorless drama expert in London once lammed into for having no form, though this is a great part of their funniness. After a particularly fierce battery, I remember Simpson—a schoolmaster, to boot, who could have run rings of logic around the drama expert if he had been moved to—sitting on the floor with his back against my hi-fi and saying, his long face no more melancholy than usual, that the man was perfectly right, that the plays had no shape at all. "It struck me at the time that I could have given them a shape," he said. "But it seemed like breaking faith with chaos."

"This question of perfection," said Renoir. "Bogus symmetry. It is one of the reasons modern objects are so ugly. Plates, dresses, colors. If you take the blue of faïence, the blue of delft, it is never absolutely pure, you see. There is nothing quite pure in nature. In the Army, with the cavalry, I learned that there are no white horses and no black horses. They always have a number of hairs that are another color. If the horses were plastic, that would be an unforgivable fault. My father used to talk about this idea. Not about plastic, of course. . . . He had, for example, a small piece of advice for young architects. He said to them that they might think of destroying their perfect tools and replacing the symmetry produced by their instruments with the symmetry produced by their own eye. When he was asked about a school for artists, he said he would like to see inns—inns with the temperament of English pubs—where people would be fed and where they would live and where nobody would teach them a single thing. He said that he didn't want the spirits of young artists to be tidied up. His talk was terribly interesting. Toward the end of his life he would think deeply, perhaps because he couldn't walk. I believe sitting in a wheelchair helped him to think as he did. Often I would suppose he was working, and then just find him sitting, and we would have a conversation much like the one I am having with you. A certain spectrum of life would interest him."

Renoir's cast of mind often seems very like his father's. "As the years went by, I found he was becoming rather a marble bust instead of a man," Renoir recalled. "I wanted to stop that. It was why I wrote a book about him, I think." He spoke about Auguste Renoir's attitude toward prowess, and it defined his own. He said that his father "didn't care for *tours de force*"—that "to his way of thinking, the beauty of, say, a weightlifter was at its greatest when the young man was lifting only something very light." The filmmaker son does that. The world he created in *La Règle du Jeu* spins on his forefinger. We talked about the biography. It is called *Renoir, My Father*, and he published it in 1958. I had the impression that he misses his father daily. We also talked about his books. "I like writing," he said. "Because it doesn't matter."

Another day, we went to see a film. The screenplay of the film—Truffaut's *Stolen Kisses*—he found "very interesting." He said, "It has no suspense. I hate the sanctity of suspense. It's left over from nineteenth-century romanticism. The film is to the point and comic. It is a sort of synopsis of the times, this humor. It is not so much something to laugh at as an attitude toward life that you can share. At least, in *this* film you are permitted to share it. So the film must be good, I think. I like it very much."

We walked out into the cool sun. Renoir inspected the streets and said, "It seems to me that the people of Paris are gayer than usual. Perhaps it's the weather? ["*Il a une telle correspondance avec la nature*," Sylvia Bataille had said a few days before.] Or perhaps it's still the effect of the events of May in 1968." He looked closely at everything, as if he were going to draw it from memory later.

The taxi we took had a postcard of a Picasso stuck in the dashboard: inevitably, in Renoir's company, it seemed. He instantly leaned forward and started to talk about it. The driver, who chatted with hair-raising responsiveness in the Paris traffic, turned out to be a spare-time painter. "Only to amuse myself, you understand," he said.

"Why not?" said Renoir. "Everything interesting is only to amuse yourself."

The driver, making the taxi lurch horribly, produced a magazine called *Science & Art*. We nearly hit something because he was finding a page to show Renoir and then stabbing a forefinger at the place, leaning over to the back seat with his eyes on the magazine. "Paintings by madmen," the driver explained during a feat with the clutch and the accelerator.

Renoir looked at the page and exclaimed. It showed a schizophrenic's painting, a gilded dream of a Madonna and Child that also had something carnal and pagan about it, like a Bonnard, and something quite free, as things tend to be in Renoir's presence.

The two men talk with passionate absorption about, in turn, madmen, the Madonna, and paintbrushes. As we get out, the driver gives Renoir the magazine, shakes his hand, and offers his name.

"Renoir," responds Renoir, and he thanks the driver for the present as he climbs out, his bad leg slowing him a little.

"You are of the family Renoir?" says the driver, amazed, moved, something dawning on him, looking at Renoir's face.

"Yes."

"Of the painter Renoir?"

"Yes. He was my father."

The driver goes on looking. "You are yourself, then . . . There was a famous man of the theater and the cinema . . ."

"That's my nephew Claude. A cameraman. Or my brother Pierre, perhaps. The actor."

"No, someone some time ago, a most famous man of the theater and the cinema, I believe."

"Yes, I think you are right, I believe there was once another Renoir who worked in the theater. Not related."

When we were pottering about the kitchen one day at lunchtime, Renoir said severely, "We will not have much. You don't eat, and now I don't eat, either. You must have been easy to ration," and he started talking about the Second World War. He was very kind to the English, even to the food. "Without the English, we should now all be under the jackboot. Yorkshire pudding, Lancashire hot pot. Exactly how is shepherd's pie made?" Just before the fall of Paris, Renoir and Dido joined the flight to the Midi. He took with him some of the most treasured paintings in the world. His own car was in the country, far away. "I didn't know what to do," he said. "At last, it occurred to me: perhaps one can still hire a car. Perhaps the Peugeot people are still working. So we went to the Peugeot factory, and there is every clerk at work as usual, still filling out forms, with the Germans ten miles away. I have to fill out all these forms, and then we have a car, and we drive to the Midi, very slowly, with the canvases of Monsieur Cézanne, et cetera, in the back. A big trek to the south. Everyone who could find a cart or a wheelbarrow. It was a very bad sight."

Renoir has his father's strong respect for touch, and for a kind of conviviality that is unmistakable and moving when he creates it in any of his films. He is a fine friend to spend time with. "One of the things I like about Shakespeare, very much, is that the characters have a great variety of intimacy," he said to me. "They are different according to whom they are speaking to. Of course, Shakespeare had a great advantage over cinema directors. It is one that in-

terests me a lot. He shares it with, you could say, Simenon.
You could call it the advantage of a harness. Elizabethan
plays and also thrillers are constricted, and that is very
liberating. In the cinema, you can do all too much. For
example, when the hero of a modern film has a phobia, you
are obliged to explain it by flashbacks: I mean, to go back to
the time when he was beaten by his father, or whatever thing
is supposed to have had such a result. This freedom can be
quite enfeebling. It makes one very literal, very anxious to
make everything clear, get everything taped. You know, I
believe one has to have only a rough idea when one is
making a film or writing a story, or whatever. A rough
scheme, like a salmon going upstream. No more than that.
It's no true help—is it?—to know already where one is going
to arrive. In fact, I think targets have done a great deal of
harm. This nineteenth-century idea in Europe, and now in
America—this idea of targets—has caused terrible damage.
Rewards in the future, and so on. Those never come. Pen-
sions. I thought about this a good deal in India when I was
making *The River*, in 1949 and 1950. India was a revelation. I
suppose I'd been looking for such a place and thinking it was
all past, and there it was. Suppose you are interested in
Aristophanes, and suppose you go down the street and
suddenly see people who are exactly his contemporaries,
who know the same things, have the same view. That's what
India was like for me. I had been starting to fall off to sleep.
In India, you could make a full-length picture just by following someone through the day. A grandmother, say, getting
up in the morning, cooking, washing clothes. Everything
noble. Among poor people in India, you're surrounded by
an aristocracy and a nobility. The trouble now is that the
advanced countries are trying desperately to grow better by

the mistaké of removing the ordinary. We're trying to reach greatness by reading classics in houses that have no cold in the winter and no heat in the summer, and where everything can be done without the natural waste of time. One of the things I liked about India is that the people have the secret of loitering." This brought up Los Angeles, the city famous for picking up as a vagrant anyone who is merely strolling along a street. Renoir was very firm. "All great civilizations have been based on loitering," he said.

Much later, coming back to this point after a loop of talk about food and operetta, Renoir said, "Think of the Greeks, for instance. One of the most interesting adventures in our history. What were the Greeks doing in the agora? Loitering. Not getting agoraphobia. The result is Plato. My film *Boudu* is the story of a man who is just loitering."

Renoir spoke of Satyajit Ray, his helper on *The River,* whose Indian films are much like the ones that Renoir had just envisioned for me, and who feels Renoir and *The River* to be vital inspirations of his own work. "He is quite alone, of course. Most other Indian films are—well, I suppose they would be called uninteresting, though I have to say that they often interest me very much. There is sometimes a wonderful mixture of fairy tales and daily life and the religious, and no one thinks of it as at all comic, because no one is conscious of incongruity. I saw this in an Italian theater once. A little theater, not much bigger than this room. At the front of the stage, a man threatening to kill his mother. In the back, by some trick, a locomotive rushing. It was very fine. Hamlet and railway stations. Genuinely popular. You know what I mean. Every now and then, one gets this in Indian films. In the middle of a story about Siva and a film star and dancing and so on, there will suddenly be a god with a mustache who looks like a cop. It is practically the only question of the age, this question of primitivism and how it can be sustained in the face of sophistication. It is the question of Vietnam."

This question is much on his mind, and he came back to it another day by another route. "You know, I have a theory about the decay of art in advanced civilizations," he said. "Perhaps it's a joke, but I believe it may be serious. It is that people *want* to make ugly things, but at the beginning their tools don't allow them to. When you find figures or vases in Mycenae or Guatemala or Peru, every one is a masterpiece. But when the perfection of technique allows men to do what they want, it is bad. Perfection of technique —sophistication—has nearly destroyed the movies. In the beginning, every movie was good. When we see the old silents at the Cinémathèque, they are all good. This isn't nostalgia. They are. And, believe me, I know some of the directors who made them and they aren't geniuses. It also has something to do with puritanısm. I'm in favor of puritanism, I think. Not for me. But for a nation it can be very good, and for art. Those early movies in Hollywood reflected the decorum of the people, a kind of thinking that I could not abide for myself. We would demonstrate against it now, I daresay, including me. You know what I think about all this? I believe that Creation has a considerable sense of humor. Of farce. The closer we are to perfection, the farther away from it we are. This makes me think about Hollywood, of course. The interesting thing about Hollywood, Beverly Hills, Los Angeles is that it isn't really materialist at all—not in the true sense, because it obviously doesn't care for the material in the slightest. In fact, that's the big advantage of Hollywood: the fact that the buildings don't count. It is therefore a place in the abstract. You are there—no, I should say that *one* is there, and I suppose I must mean myself—only for one's friends. When Clifford Odets died, I thought I wanted to leave Hollywood. He was a prince. Every gesture, every way of thinking was noble. Although I love Hollywood, I have to say that it is without nobility. But I stayed, of course. You know what I like about America? Among other things, the obvious. The generosity. There is a great desire to share. To share feelings, to share friends. Of course, this can be a travesty and ridiculous. It can be reduced to 'togetherness' and the vocabulary that could find such a word for such a thing. But it also has to be said that there exists in America a stout attempt to do in language exactly the opposite, to make things noble. For instance, calling tea a beverage, calling a barber a hairdresser. It doesn't work, but the attempt, in the face of the obstacles—well, it's interesting and nice, isn't it? It is very much harder to live nobly in America than in India. One of the things that are helpful to Indians is the concept of privacy. It is so strong there that to have spiritual privacy they do not even need physical privacy. In America, this concept is not so easy to have, partly because of the ethic of sharing, perhaps, and partly because of the ethic of proselytizing and persuading other people, which Hinduism is entirely free of, and which has arrived so dreadully at Vietnam for America. The problem of caste—of Western caste, of paternalism, et cetera—has led us into this proselytizing. I suppose caste is what all my films are about. Still, any big society is a melting pot, as they say. Take Rome. And the banal melting pot of America that is so much in question at the moment really works pretty well except at one point. The point of the Negro. One forgets that the slaves weren't originally brought by the Americans. They were brought by the French, the Spanish, the Portuguese. The really difficult thing to explain is that the slave owners pretended to be Christians. All men are brothers, and in the meantime the brothers on your estate are slaves. I suppose it has to be recognized that much of the truth about Christianity is about money, and most of the truth about subjection and propaganda is about money. Outside Paris now, there are Arabs living in shacks built out of gasoline cans who make a great deal of money for Paris businessmen. Americans make money out of Negroes, and Frenchmen make money out of Arabs. Every country has a worm in the apple, and the worm in the apple of America is a very tough one."

We went out into the Place Pigalle. "Much changed since the days of my father and Monsieur Cézanne," Renoir said, perfectly cheerfully. There was a night club on the corner which had the present special tattiness of the recently new. "Sensass!" a placard said of a stripper. The whole place was plastered with the words of some arid new Esperanto. "Chinese," Renoir said firmly. "A Chinese dialect that is understood only on this side of the square."

He talked about his new novel. It is about a murder, and based on a real crime that he heard of as a small child from Gabrielle, his father's famous model. It happened in a village between Burgundy and Champagne. "Two murderers," he said. "One with a big nose, the leader, and the other the weak one. At the time of the murder, which was very terrible, the villagers heard the sound of the ax blows on the earth to bury the corpse. The earth was very cold. The sounds seemed to them to be coming from under the earth. That was the way Gabrielle remembered them. They came from the private cemetery. Somebody seemed to be trying to escape from the ground, everyone thought. The cemetery

had been made for a man in the French Revolution who
didn't want to be buried in a religious place." A while later,
considering what the story might be like as a film, he said,
"Too violent. I'm an admirer of violent films, but I can't
make them. Also, I am scared of them." He was about to
spend five days or a week in the country where the murder
happened. The name of the village—very near his own
family region—is Gloire-Dieu. Someone had sent him a
browned clipping of a local song about the crime, which he
said had deeply wounded the villagers' sense of blessedness
in their name:

COMPLAINTE SUR LE CRIME DE LA GLOIRE-DIEU

Écoutez la triste histoire
Désolant notre pays.
En faisant le récit,
Vraiment on ne peut y croire,
Car le pays bourguignon
N'a pas un mauvais roman . . .

Renoir talked about a lot of other plans. Some that had
been scotched seemed no particular cue for regret. The
ideas continued to interest him, and it was sometimes quite
hard to be sure whether he was describing a plan of his own
or the plot of some favorite already achieved: the "Satyri-
con" of Petronius, for one. He recited the stories of classics
in the present tense, and they acquired his own tang. "There
is this matron who lost her husband, and she is so much in
love she can't bear the thought of being alone," he said,
limping along the cobbles and helping me. "She stays in the
cemetery near the corpse of her husband. There is a soldier
nearby who is watching thieves. The crucified bodies of
thieves. The authorities have to have a soldier there, because

one thief's family wants to steal the body. The soldier says to
the woman, 'Don't cry so loud,' and he comforts her so well
that after two or three days he makes love, and the family
can steal the corpse, and so everyone is happier, except that
the soldier has failed in his official task and what on earth
can he do?"

Without changing his tone, Renoir went on from Petronius to describe his unmade film about revolt. He had
written it in two parts. At no time did he speak of it in the
past. "One is a revolt against an electric waxing machine.
The other is about war. Two corporals from two armies hide
between enemy lines beneath the roof of a kind of cellar. We
start with a very polite fight about who will be the prisoner of
the other one. In the end, they decide there is only one
decent position in the modern world and that is to be a
prisoner. But each doesn't like the enemy food. Oh, and
now I have suddenly found the ending, in talking to you. I
think this is the ending. They change uniforms, and then
each can be the prisoner of the other and have the food he
likes."

The television show he is doing is "like a revue." He
continues, "Some of the sketches are very short—no more
than a sentence. There is one sketch of the Armistice, and a
burglar breaks a vein in his neck and wakes a sleepwalker
and they are the first victims of the peace. Before this, there
is a soldier who is told by a sergeant that if he dies before the
Armistice he will be right and if he dies after the Armistice
he will be wrong. You know what has happened? Patriotism
is really quite a new idea to the ordinary citizen. It happens
to be useful in politics to pretend that it is a powerful emotion, but it isn't. Not widely. Most people have never thought
first of their country; they've thought first of their family.

You know, I adore England. I have English relatives. I'd like to live there. People live there very agreeably." (Though I should think he could live anywhere, given friends, just as he can make enjoyable work for himself in strange countries or in atrocious circumstances.)

"The trouble is that techniques change and the actors' style of playing changes," he said. "Just as fashions vanish, so our films go into oblivion to join others that once moved us."

The greatest of Renoir's will never do this, but he doesn't seem to know it. It makes you pause to see a man with such a powerful sense of the continuity of the general life engaged with the form that most deals in quick deaths. He eludes that blow by understanding filmmaking another way, as play. He will sometimes describe a director as "*le meneur de jeu,*" and he calls his friends and collaborators his accomplices. "The cinema uses things up very fast. That's the point," he says. "It uses up ideas and people and kinds of stories, and all the time it thinks it wants to be new. It has no idea that film people themselves change and are new all the time. Producers want me to make the pictures I made twenty years ago. Now I am someone else. I have gone away from where they think I am."

PARIS, 1968

Concerning 11 Films

Salute to Mayhem:
Boudu Sauvé des Eaux (1932)

BOUDU SAUVÉ DES EAUX, shows disruption triumphant. Michel Simon in the part of Boudu, the haywire tramp whose vision of the way life should be anticipates the hippies' by nearly forty years, gives it a curious benediction through Renoir's filmmaking genius. At the beginning of the film, Boudu has lost his dog. A policeman brushes aside his request for help. Boudu is not a lovable tramp. He is nothing like Chaplin. When he attempts to commit suicide by drowning, a bookseller saves him and tries to rehabilitate him in his own house, but there is nothing doing. The bookseller's kindly aim is to turn the unruly man into a good bourgeois like himself, but Boudu prefers to be left alone. He doesn't want to be saved. There is no place in society that he covets. If this is the world, he would rather be out of it. He does his best to impel the move, by saying with a chortle that he doesn't absolutely *need* an offered necktie, by pursuing the bookseller's mistress (who is the housemaid), by seducing his wife, by saying that the sheets make him sweat ("I get sick"), and by taking firmly to the bookseller's floor.

The film, written by Renoir and Albert Valentin from a minor play of the time, is a lyric and riotous account of a dissident who escapes by a system of mayhem. He wants none of the things that respectability wants him to want. While the wife grows petulant in the kitchen, he lies down on his shoulder blades and props up a doorjamb with his carpet slippers, says he suspects that the bookseller fished him out of the drink because he needed a servant, and spits genially onto a first edition of Balzac. The wife, dusting herself with talcum powder, mutters distractedly that her nerves are going to crack. It is obvious to her that one should rescue only people of one's own class. Michel Simon's loose, doggy face, visible in typical Renoir shots through a spiral staircase and in distant rooms as he concocts worrying schemes, incites the wife to spite: "I can only shun the man who spat on Balzac." To her horror, he not only makes love to her, which stays well within the bounds of what she finds socially acceptable, but goes as far as to call her by her first name. Her husband is slightly mollified by getting a medal for the rescue. Meanwhile, Boudu intones *Les Fleurs du Mal* in the doorway and smokes an obviously smelly cigar. The film comes full circle when he marries the maid and sets out in a bowler hat with his bride in a boat. Nearly trapped in a social act, he throws himself into the river. Not suicide. Not despair. An escape from what is expected of him. Barking and rolling like a sea lion, he floats slowly down the river and eventually hauls himself up onto a bank, staggering drunkenly and embracing a scarecrow as though it were a colleague. There is a three-hundred-and-sixty-degree shot of the free world regained, and then the camera sinks down to the grass and the white dust raised by a breeze in the summer heat. You can have seen the film fifteen years ago and still remember that grass, that dust, that freedom.

Locked Out of a Golden Circle: Toni (1935)

VIEWED IN HISTORICAL context or not, *Toni* is still one of the most remarkable achievements of realism in the cinema. Renoir never beats the drum. His method of shooting and of directing actors is always to leave air around them. He is interested in people's actions less than in their reactions, interested in scenes less than in the actors moving about in them, interested in whole scenarios less than in scenes.

He shot this film in the Midi, without makeup, studio sets, or stars. The cameraman was his nephew Claude. The film, which is transformed by Renoir's characteristic beneficence, began with his equally characteristic simplicity as a dossier on a *crime passionnel*. The story is about Toni, an Italian immigrant who comes to France to find work (your country is where you can eat), and about the two women who love him. He has a long-lasting affair with his landlady, Marie, and a thwarted one with a Spanish girl called Josepha, who marries a Belgian farmer from the quarry where Toni works. The composition of the shots of men working the quarry looks very like Bruegel's "Tower of Babel." The film is full of wonderfully exact observations: the sense of a dying relationship in bedroom scenes between Toni and Marie, a baby howling during a quarrel about money in a poor kitchen, the sounds of motorbike engines, and a funeral bell and a guitar intervening disconnectedly on the track.

Toni is a monument to Renoir's undying preoccupation with meetings and intruders. How to enter, how to belong. Again and again, in many different films, he has asked the same question: what happens to strangers in milieus that are not theirs? And alongside this question, which must lead always to explosions (in *La Règle du Jeu*, for instance, and even in *Diary of a Chambermaid*, the finest film of his Hollywood exile during the war, though it is constrained by the presence of stars, the then alien language, and the even more alien studio sets)—alongside this there is the pacifying effect of the details of side-life, which have the balm of the manifold and prodigious.

Boon Nights:
Le Crime de Monsieur Lange
(1935)

RENOIR WAS BORN in 1894, so he was twenty in 1914, but it seems that the stop that was then put to the world's sense of *douceur de vivre* never happened to him. He has survived every derangement and bleakness of the century. I don't believe one enjoys Mozart because of the arrangements of the notes; as Renoir once said of someone else, you enjoy yourself because you have a good conversation with Mozart. After seeing other and mediocre films, *Le Crime de Monsieur Lange* is like friendship after days of trivia on the telephone. Renoir has a particular view of life—some plenitude of spirit—that is vivacious and reviving, particularly at moments in the history of this planet when ground seems sorely lost. Without sacrificing shrewdness, he really does believe that people have a tendency to move on. His characters are always peculiarly alert, as if he never failed to sense in others a wish to find out more. The atmosphere in *Monsieur Lange* made me remember something he said when he was on location in India after Independence, directing *The River*. He looked at the fighting then going on between Hindus and Muslims and said only that they had not yet caught up with the times.

I suppose *Le Crime de Monsieur Lange* couldn't be called his most important film, if that means much. It isn't as shapely or powerful a masterpiece as *La Grande Illusion* or *La Règle du Jeu*, but the same man made it, and this very man would forgo such tape measuring. It is suffused with light and the possibility of happiness and a sense that life is simultaneously serious, absurd, impossible, and inescapably interesting. He made the film in the Depression. It has a simple plot. It amounts to a fable about capitalism, to a caustic revenge farce, to an idyll, and to a stingingly undeceived tale about being near the bottom of the heap. Renoir has created a Brechtian narrative that is also pastoral and bitten with fugacity, and filled every shot with flickering notations of living.

The picture begins with a flash-forward of lovers on the run. The man, Monsieur Lange, is technically guilty of murder, though the murder was poetically justified, and it can't be long before he is captured; but he still has left to him a pause to love his girl, and the grace of reprieve flows back from this scene over the rest of the picture. He is played by René Lefèvre, the star of René Clair's *Le Million*. At the beginning of the story proper, we see him spending as much time as possible in bed, writing Wild West stories that nobody reads. His employer, Batala (Jules Berry), is a foppishly dressed embezzler who publishes junk magazines, starves his employees, and farcically deceives his backers. There is one scene that has a vivacity very like the temperament of Restoration comedy, with Batala sidestepping the inquiries of an equally courtly backer who has been under the impression that the firm would be publishing wholesome books called "Hymn to Work" and "Whither Are We Drifting?"—the backer's idea being that these holy bromides for the underfed should include a few plugs for some pills called Ranimax.

Batala diverts the furious but dapper enemy with questions about the man's inappropriately amiable little dog.

"It's called Daisy," the investor says impatiently.

"That's an English name, isn't it?" asks the embezzler.

"*Belgian*," snaps the investor, trying to edge nearer to a mannerly suggestion that the word "swindle" is applicable.

Batala suddenly has an idea involving the neglected Lange. It is his stroke of impresario's genius. He says, grabbing air, that the Wild West Stories are in a class with *Les Misérables*. His mind races. He can adapt Lange's hero in *Arizona Jim* to push the pills. "Just imagine, Don Quixote taking Ranimax pills. . . ." The author raptly signs his rights away.

Batala is capable of exploiting anyone. He sends off his own mistress to content a creditor. Toward sceptical employees in the printing office he behaves like a patronizing kindergarten teacher. He tells them how to draw. The corpse should show, he feels. And there should be more detail. "Remember, a crime is full of small details," he says, patting the neck of a man who would like his blood, or at least a living wage. (All the dialogue scenes go very swiftly. Every now and then, the camera moves down to a yard below the office, where children play and dogs look for food, and an unseen church bell rings. It is characteristic of Renoir, this way of giving you the sense of time passing in a place at the margin of incident.) Batala eventually goes too far, and the creditors nearly nab him. Having committed every crime of the soul, he climbs onto a train where he talks indignantly with a priest about the immorality of the age and disappears. *Arizona Jim* turns into a hit, the publishing office becomes a cooperative, and Lange's flower-faced girl friend loves him. There is a rhapsodic feast. "Every time I'm drunk, I think it's Christmas," a nearly unconscious worker shouts cheerfully. Then Batala reappears, alive and kicking and disguised in the priest's vestments, after the train accident that was supposed to have killed him. It is too much to be borne. It means the end of the co-op, and a plumper Batala than ever. Lange takes his revenge, and the end of the film links back to the beginning. He and his girl still have a little freedom left. The last long shot of them, pushing their luck in some plundered interlude, has a kind of piercing beauty that mysteriously belongs more to comedy than to tragedy, like the racking supposition of Falstaff that his boon nights with Hal are going to go on forever.

Renoir wrote the story with Jean Castanier—"a spherical Catalan friend . . . who spent most of his time getting drunk on the air of the Paris suburbs," as the director described him in 1961. (Jacques Prévert wrote the screenplay.) Renoir had another crony at the time, Carl Koch, who was the husband of the animator Lotte Reiniger and became his collaborator on *La Grande Illusion*. Koch had nothing directly to do with *Monsieur Lange*, but Renoir drew him into the description of things to me, all the same: "Our strolls on the banks of the Seine were favorable to the birth of a story. Sometimes Bert Brecht got off the boat with one or two friends. A young woman would unwrap a concertina from its newspaper . . ."

Renoir's talk is very like his films. Things happen, people come and go, all belong. No wonder he responded to Hinduism when he made *The River*. "The great word of the Hindu . . . is that the world is one," he said in an interview with Jacques Rivette and François Truffaut soon after-

wards. "This does not mean an acceptance in the Moham-
medan manner, a kind of fatalism. The single man can act.
Nevertheless, you cannot undo what has been done. . . . It is
a sort of comprehension by the senses of everything that has
happened." This is the morality that pours out of his films. It
is a morality of bearing witness.

Flophouse:
Les Bas-Fonds (1936)

THERE EXISTS a rare old Russian screen record of Gorky's *The Lower Depths* as it was played long ago by the Moscow Arts Theatre, with the great Kachalov, now dead, as the Baron. Renoir's marvellous *Les Bas-Fonds* of years later is interestingly different. The Moscow Arts picture is entirely Russian in the wit, the buffoonery, the richness of idiosyncrasy, the profusion of swollen, hallucinated faces, dreaming and condemned. Renoir's version has Louis Jouvet in the Kachalov part and remains entirely French, where any other director would have tried to confect Russianness. "Bresson has said that originality is when you try to do the same as everybody else but don't quite make it," Renoir once remarked to me, apropos of something quite different. The flophouse in his *Les Bas-Fonds*—built around one of the courtyards he loves—is unconsciously just as much Renoir's original issue as Gorky's. Renoir's character is all there in the film: in the response to a story about a dandy who has been stripped by the bailiffs and fallen among guttersnipes who recognize and fear his class; in the minute social sense; in the bitter tenderness; and in the breath of temperament and curiosity that fills the frames of any Renoir film with unmistakable liveliness. He begins with a long shot on Jouvet, the debonair Baron in military uniform, hearing out a voice-over lecture from a superior officer about debts. The shot is held daringly, as Godard often holds one now. In the Baron's palatial home, run by a sadly grateful, class-conscious servant who is never going to get his back wages, a burglar played by Jean Gabin comes in to pinch the valuables and sits down with the Baron to a comradely glass of champagne on tick. The Baron knows what is going to happen to his life, like everyone else in his circle. He has squandered a fortune. In the gambling rooms, his unamiable friends can always tell when he has lost: he walks out calmly enough with a cigarette, but it is unlit, whereas he unconsciously lights it if he has won. The slope now leads only downward, and he already knows himself to be in Gabin's shoes. When he gets to the flophouse, after leaving his empty mansion and his unpaid servant with an air, he finds himself at an irreparable distance from everyone else there. Gabin leans on an elbow in a field and talks to him, in a way that he can't quite recognize, about being fed up. "The mattresses . . . saucepans . . . every word that is spoken is rotten to the core," Gabin says, talking beside a river with a grass-blade in his mouth, in one of the interludes that Renoir directs as no one else can. The Baron and the burglar have escaped for the moment from the flophouse: from the girls desperate to get married as a way out, from the jammy-mouthed government inspector promising to make a princess of one of the down-and-outs if she will have dinner with him, from the crazed alcoholic actor who sees visions of a cure. The Baron has disabused the drunk of those visions, and the drunk has hit back: "You're a real baron. Even with holes in your shoes, you're destructive." Lying with Gabin on the bank, the Baron says that everything in his life has seemed like a dream, consisting mostly of

changing clothes—beginning with being a schoolboy, then
being married, then a government official—and he looks
down at his tramp's coat, the sleeves ending four inches
above his wrists.

Les Bas-Fonds is unmistakably Renoir's. He shot in deep
focus long before Orson Welles and Gregg Toland, because
he wants to see everything in motion at the same time and
because he prefers not to commandeer your eye. He always
likes to see what is going on in the next room, through
half-open doors, or across a courtyard, so his compositions
often have the tunnelling perspectives of the great Flemish
interior paintings. The scenario of the film was presented to
him by Jacques Companeez and Eugène Zamiatin, and he
responded to it at once. The adaptation and the dialogue are
by Renoir himself, with Charles Spaak, who later collabo-
rated with him on La Grande Illusion. He seems always to
have been interested by the idea of a beggars' kingdom, like
Gay, Brecht, and Weill before him. More than this, his
version of the Gorky play becomes, through his temperament and intellect, a heartrending poem about the loss of
caste. The delicate comprehension it proffers to the resolves
and wounds of class that are often made light of now by
progressive film directors puts it thematically with La Règle
du Jeu and La Grande Illusion, his two masterpieces. (And,
indeed, with practically every other film he has ever made.
He said to me recently, about another director, "Probably
everyone makes only one film in his life, and then smashes it
into pieces and makes it again.") Renoir's feeling in Les Bas-
Fonds for the fop deposed, for the grandee who has lost his
birthright in high style and will always be mistrusted by his
new familiars for that very stylishness, expresses the ideas
and the love that led him to his greatest works.

Plight of a King:
La Marseillaise (1938)

In La Marseillaise Louis XVI is played by Pierre Renoir, Jean's brother. He is a monarch much moved by culinary thoughts. Far from being asleep after what are referred to as the Herculean labors of his hunt the day before, he is first seen busy with a colossal breakfast in bed, with chicken fat running up the sleeves of his nightshirt as he eats what looks to be a whole chicken and swigs wine as if it were soda water for a headache. He is told by La Rochefoucauld-Liancourt that the Parisians have taken the Bastille. "Ah," he says intelligently, the royal mouth full. "Is it a revolt?" "No, Sire, it is a revolution," says La Rochefoucauld-Liancourt. Outside, the peasants scent freedom. They kill blackbirds with a sling. Someone laughs hoarsely about the burning of the rich, making a dissenter say gravely, almost to himself, that the nobles have taught bad habits and that they have created their slaves in their own image. Renoir finds it inapt of us to try to make things stay in place when everything is always naturally in motion. The films of this born innovator dart with life on the move. In any frame, there always seems to be something happening apart from the major point of dramatic attention. Renoir's characteristic deep-focus lens uses doorways almost as proscenium arches for stages filled with activity. In La Marseillaise he brings his usual native affection to bear on

the plight of the rigid. There is a fine scene showing
homesick nobles in Koblenz, daydreaming of the common
people still kneeling back in France. One patrician sings at
the spinet, two play cards, another fiddles with a yo-yo like a
lunatic dauphin. "Now we are the allies of Prussia. I once
met His Majesty the King of Prussia," says a beauty who
looks like a crinoline-lady cover to be put over a teapot. "An
Agamemnon . . . two hundred and eighty pounds." Meanwhile, a nobleman named Saint-Laurent remembers the
new concept of nationhood which was given him by Arnaud,
the man who deprived him of his noble position. "And yet
he was a gentleman," Saint-Laurent goes on to recall. "Yet
he was a patriot. If there are many like him, we shall not have
an easy time." Politically speaking, we are watching men
struggling to discover the wheel. Only Renoir could make
the struggle graceful, comic, and courageous: a documentary of crass primitivism and muddle which somehow,
paradoxically, expresses divine sensibility and equilibrium.
He treats peasants and emigrant courtiers with equal dignity
and respect and a deal of humor. There is a very funny
exchange between the King and Marie Antoinette about the
brushing of teeth. Louis approves of the novelty: "I will
gladly attempt this toothbrushing."

Mishaps and irrelevancies appeal to Renoir. On the
road from Marseilles, the volunteers exchange irritable
theories about what to do for sore feet. "A pair of roomy
boots packed out with straw," says one to his insteps tenderly. Another says, "Paper." Another says, "Tallow rubbed
between the toes." There are complaints that the song "La
Marseillaise" is full of unpronounceable words. An ex-
hausted enthusiast says quietly that he "likes the lines that a
schoolteacher wrote: 'We'll replace our parents on the

battlefield.' " The terse, slangy talk is all of a piece with Louis's compliments to the lately introduced tomato. Where Saint-Laurent sees the passing of an élite, Louis says the tragedy is that unfortunately the members of the court are the actors in this drama, "which is obviously less convenient than being the spectators." It is inconvenient, too, for the passionate speaker at the meeting of the Tribunes in *La Marseillaise* that she is a woman. "Your place is in the galley!" a heckler shouts.

Heredity:
La Bête Humaine (1938)

TRUFFAUT ONCE SAID to me that Renoir has a sort of "trade secret." He meant the trade secret of sympathy. Renoir degrades no one. His vein of affection makes one think of Octave, the character played by Renoir himself in *La Règle du Jeu*, who says, "You see, in this world there is one awful thing, and that is that everyone has his reasons." Renoir would accord reasons even to the accepted kind of heroism, though he reacts against it almost as strongly as he does against the Renaissance, which he identifies—in his beautiful introduction to André Bazin's book about him—as the movement that "laid the foundations of industrial society" and was "ultimately responsible for the atomic bomb."

Bazin records that, after a few years of what Renoir cheerfully pronounced to me to be utterly rotten pictures, the director resolved to study French gesture as it is reflected in his father's paintings. "I was beginning to realize that the movement of a scrubwoman, of a vegetable vender, or of a girl combing her hair before a mirror frequently had superb plastic value." His films from then on have always been full of shots of frozen action which seem to come from Impressionist paintings. In *Le Caporal Epinglé*, a small, shy child in a silent German crowd raises a hand muffled in a woolen mitten to ranks of passing French prisoners. In *La Bête Humaine*, one of the very best Renoir films, adapted from Zola without the novel's rhetoric and, ironically, without its falsely "cinematic" scheme, Jean Gabin plays a locomotive engineer. (The story is that the film got started because Gabin had always wanted to drive a train.) There is an abundance of gesture between him and his fireman, signifying unity in a clamor that no words can be heard in. The Gabin character comes from a long line of drunkards. Himself a teetotaller, he is gripped by moments of sadness that move him to an intolerable self-hatred. He begins to think he is paying for all his ancestors who drank, and gives himself pathological fits far worse than alcoholism. In a calm between storms, he throws two quick glances at his reflection in a looking glass. The contempt in his eyes is like the gaze of a basilisk. No one is better at this sort of grim, drained detail than Gabin, a Renoir actor if there ever was one. Renoir likes everything—even in his comedies and deliberately theatrical pieces—to be quick, dry: sec. Gabin's two glances are like stones hurled at a prison wall to bounce back and wound the prisoner.

Renoir has always been struck and stirred by the closed worlds that some people think they have to live in: a little series of glass cubes and spheres from which they can see other people, wave to them, copy them. The glass boxes devised by the technocrats who have so constrained liberty are prisons too low to stand in and too small to lie down in. They are torture chambers as minute as the primitive kind of prison called little-ease, but not so small as to prevent the inhabitants from grandiloquent posturing. Heredity can be wondrous, as it is for Renoir himself, who speaks again and again of his father as though the famous painter were still alive; in *La Bête Humaine*, though, heredity is another little-ease. Natural enough that the Gabin character should work on trains. They are a metaphor for his life, which runs on tracks and is sometimes catastrophically derailed. And the heroine pushes him to kill in a way that destroys his ownership of his soul. The prison in *La Grande Illusion* is made spacious by the two main characters' equality of calling. The German von Rauffenstein and the French de Boïeldieu are both aristocrats of the heart, enemies allied in sensibility. Renoir extends his devotion to those lords of inner liberty, though in his films they are more generally to be found among the populace than among the nobility. In *La Bête Humaine*, the one free man is Cabuche, the poacher—played by Renoir himself—who foreshadows the poacher in *La Règle du Jeu*. Poachers leap walls; owners hang back for form's sake, so that the rest of their party can catch up. The poacher has a sense of himself; the owners have a sense only of how they look to others. For Renoir, the master of acting movement as well as camera movement, gait expresses the difference between freedom and slavery in a second. In *La Marseillaise*, for instance, the volunteers marching from Marseilles to Paris walk like tired Boy Scouts; the palace guards move like chorus girls.

Game Without Umpire:
La Règle du Jeu (1939)

RENOIR'S LA RÈGLE DU JEU is one of the few sophisticated films about love that achieve irony without the stain of malignity. It is a work to be put with *Così Fan Tutte* and *The Marriage of Figaro*. Society is satirized with Mozart's own mixture of biting good sense and blithe, transforming acceptance. Like the operas, the film has a prodigality that is moving in itself. Fugitive moments of genius pass unstressed, because there is always infinitely more to draw upon, in the way of those Mozart melodies that disappear after one statement instead of spinning themselves out into the classic a-b-a aria form. The serene amplitude of Renoir's view floods the plot and turns it into something else. He thought at the time, in 1939, that he was making an anti-Fascist warning film in the guise of a story about a contemporary houseparty. Mozart probably had an equivalent feeling when he was setting da Ponte's librettos. The script of the film, by Renoir himself, with Carl Koch, was written with actual memories of eighteenth-century plays in mind, and it opens with a quotation from Beaumarchais.

Even for a masterpiece (masterpieces generally have savage voyages), the film has had a hard and strange history. It was made in the conditions following Munich. The opening in Paris, during the summer of 1939, was received with fury. Renoir saw one man in the audience start to burn a

newspaper in the hope of setting fire to the cinema. Because
of the presence in the cast of the Jewish actor Marcel Dalio
and the Austrian refugee Nora Grégor, the film was at-
tacked by both the anti-Semitic and the chauvinist press.
Butcher cuts were made. In October of 1939, it was banned
by the government as demoralizing. Both the Vichy and the
German Occupation authorities upheld the ban throughout
the war. Until 1956, it seemed that only the mutilated version of the film was extant. Then two young French cinema
enthusiasts who had acquired the rights to the film found
hundreds of boxes of untouched footage in a warehouse.
After two years of editing, under Renoir's supervision, they
were able to reconstruct his original film. When it was first
shown again publicly, I saw someone who had worked on it
originally sitting there with tears running down his cheeks at
the sight of it restored.

The plot is a pattern of three triangles—two of them
above stairs, one below—seen mostly at a chateau during a
big houseparty for the shooting season. The Marquis de la
Chesnaye, played by Dalio, is a dapper man who collects
eighteenth-century clockwork toys. He has Jewish blood, as
his male servants point out behind the baize door to demonstrate that he can't be relied upon always to know the rules of
being an aristocrat. His wife, Christine, played by Nora
Grégor, is a high-bred Austrian woman, frightened to find
herself fond of an aviator who has just flown solo across the
Atlantic and let out an angry declaration of love to her at Le
Bourget during a radio interview. This is one of the triangles.
The second is made up of the Marquis, his wife, and his
mistress, a dark, overanimated society girl whose most sober
thought is that she wants to be happy; she says it sadly two or
three times during the film, between spasms of social chat-

ter. "How are your factories?" she gabbles brightly, blotting out pain to greet a moneyed woman at the chateau. The third triangle is formed by Schumacher, the Marquis's gamekeeper; his wife, Lisette, the Marquise's maid, who is based in Paris away from her husband and living a surrogate life because of her loyalty to her mistress; and a poacher who crosses the lines to respectability and becomes a bootboy, because the Marquis has been tepidly attracted by the fact that the man is more efficient than the gamekeeper at trapping the rabbits that lower the tone of the shoot. With Lisette's adored mistress in town so much, Schumacher feels he might as well be a widower. He tries to get the Marquis to pay heed to the problem, in a desolately comic scene on the chateau doorstep while they move between car and front door, but the Marquis has guests and rococo and rabbits on his mind. This ignored third triangle is to intersect fatally with the others when Schumacher, run amok with loss and jealousy, mistakenly kills the aviator because he thinks it is Lisette rather than the Marquise who is with him. And through it all—through the bright welcomes and the glances and the melancholy accommodations to loveless social rules, through the shooting party and the amateur theatricals and the good-night scenes in long corridors where nobly born men horse around with hunting horns while a lordlier-looking servant walks impassively past them—through the whole intricate gavotte of the film wanders the solicitous figure of Octave, played by Renoir. Octave is the external extra man, the buffoon who really has both more sense and more passion than the others of his class, the one who best loves the Marquise and pines to look after her in memory of her father, who taught him music in Austria long ago. He would have liked to be a conductor. The man whom

everyone idly holds dear for being the perfect guest suddenly speaks of himself with hatred for living the life of a
sponger. How would he eat if it were not for his friends?
The thing is to forget it and get drunk. Though then, after
feeling better, he feels worse—that's the nasty part. But he
will grow accustomed, as necessary. He used to dream of
having something to offer. Of having contact with an audience. It would have been overwhelming. . . .

The houseparty's formal shooting scene has its double
later on, in the desperately actual one when Schumacher
runs among the guests and tries to kill the poacher. The
amateur theatricals that everyone treats so seriously have
their mirror image also in this drama, which the houseparty
takes for play. The intrusion of the aviator into an alien
society—the romantic hero thrust among sceptics trained in
old rules, the pure among the impure—has its counterpart
in the poacher, catapulted into a world of snobbery-by-
proxy and of a chef's adopted airs about making potato
salad with white wine. He accepted the Marquis's offer
gratefully, because he had always dreamed of being a servant. Limited hopes, delusory debts. He had always liked the
clothes. Julien Carette plays him wonderfully. When he is
seen in the servants' hall for the first time, a vagrant corral-
led within the laws of the housebound, his right arm wheels
with embarrassment as he introduces himself. There is a
shot of him in front of a palm tree with the Marquis during
the evening fête, straightening the master's tie. "Did you
ever want to be an Arab?" asks the Marquis. They are both
thinking about women. The Marquis, with two women on
his mind, envies Arabs for not having to throw out one for
another. "I hate hurting people," he says, and he means it, in
his fashion. "Ah, but a harem takes money," says the

poacher. "If I want to have a woman, or to get rid of her, I try to make her laugh. Why don't you try it?" "That takes talent," says the Marquis.

La Règle du Jeu is delicately good to every character in it, even to the most spoiled or stilted. For its characters, driven to their limits, it has the special eye that Renoir always reserves for people nearly beyond what they can manage. There is a wonderful shot of Schumacher, the violent, rigid gamekeeper, now sacked from his job because of the shooting affair, and thus separated completely from the lady's-maid wife he was trying to save for himself. She chose to stay with Madame. He stands with his forehead against a tree, stiffly, finished, like a propped scarecrow. The game has gone wrong. The rules—for him as for the aviator —were so much dead wood, but he was deceived in hoping to hack his way back to life by violent action. For the others the game still holds, although the idea of honor has petered out into the advisability of avoiding open indiscretion, and the idea of happiness into being amused. The *crime passionnel* of the plot, terrible for all three triangles, is given the labelling of his class by the Marquis. It is called "an unfortunate accident." He tells his guests that the gamekeeper, who was actually egged on by the poacher to shoot the aviator because they thought he was poaching Lisette from them both, "fired in the course of duty" on an intruder suspected of the only kind of poaching that gamekeepers are supposed to deal with.

Like the script, the editing is everywhere immaculate. The shooting-party scene, with smocked beaters thwacking the undergrowth and a sound-track like a panicky cuckoo clock, is one of the best set pieces in the French cinema; the cuts between the preoccupied lovers and their animal victims, alike jerking with damage, are brutally apropos. Renoir's formal command of his film is beautiful. During the last part of the picture, the camera moves about almost like another guest. It must be some quality of Renoir's that makes his camera lens seem always a witness and never a voyeur. The witness here communicates a powerful mixture of amusement and dismay. *La Règle du Jeu* was made in 1939, after all; it is not only a masterpiece of film-making, not only a great work of humanism and social comedy in a perfect rococo frame, but also an act of historical testimony.

Acting:
Eléna et les Hommes (1956)

IN ELÉNA ET LES HOMMES, one of Renoir's clearest expressions of his feeling for the theater, Ingrid Bergman plays a politically infatuated Polish princess of the nineteenth century who has fallen on poorer days. Her idea of fending off poverty is to sell a pearl. The film is like a late-Shakespearean comedy of gesture and romance about a woman who believes herself dedicated to causes. She is buoyed up by a dilettante (Mel Ferrer), for whom lounge-lizardry is an art, and a general (Jean Marais), founded on the real-life Boulanger, whom the French people want to make into their presiding genius. The populace is eager to grow excited about its own dreams. Love's exhibition at the end, when Eléna is forced to appease a crowd by appearing at a balcony window with Mel Ferrer—substituting Ferrer in order to save the general from the mob—is the final stroke of theatricality, with the balcony almost playing the dividing theatrical role of footlights. The spectacle of romantic love meets a receptive audience. The crowd roars its approval of this slave of the heart, this outsider who echoes the regional Venus of Balzac's *Eugénie Grandet*. She is an emblem of real love submerged in farcically pompous and maladroit disguises. All through the film, starting with the moment when she mingles with the crowd on Bastille Day, there is a sense of movement and light irony which is pure Renoir.

The film is about the intrigues of the early years of the Third Republic. *Eléna* is a big movie in the guise of a breakable and fine-tuned little gem, with a diamond watch movement that the people in the film take to be the same tick-tock that the dropsical Fielding, laughed at for his size by the watermen at Rotherhithe, thought the activity of his own great heart to be. Impromptu, Eléna sings gloriously in a café scene, yet with the Renoir hint that there is something faintly ridiculous in bel canto: the same suspicion is embodied in the marvellous warbling of Jeanne Moreau in *Le Petit Théâtre de Jean Renoir* (1969). *Eléna et les Hommes* is the ultimate extension of Renoir's feeling for the theater. Politics are reducible to shadow plays, to romances, to crowd appearances of beauties in hats burdened with flowers; it is love and art that supply the real values. One thinks of the dramatic sense in *La Règle du Jeu,* and of the comedy about romanticism implicit in the way Mel Ferrer deals with Ingrid Bergman's difficult clothes in *Eléna et les Hommes*; for instance, avoiding the darts of the white ostrich feathers that sprout from the evening dress on her perfect shoulders, because he hopes not to be tickled into sneezing in their box at the opera. One thinks, too, of the cruel, audacious theatricality of *Le Crime de Monsieur Lange,* which is a step away from mere theater, and beyond the theater in its icily deliberate use of the stage's furthest devices of alienation, like *Les Bas-Fonds,* the fiercely melodramatic version of Gorky's *The Lower Depths.* Drama is seen by Renoir as more truthful than politics, which he depicts as a misleadingly lifelike form of staging, with the voters playing the part of an extension of the audience; a Brechtian weight of unreal emphasis on art's techniques, he feels, can embody perceptions more truly than verisimilitude. In an equally startling way, he celebrates a certain kind of very attentive sloth, as it must have been known by the brillant spectators dawdling in the Greek agora. Renoir understands this sort of inertia as the most productive form of energy: unrestless and alert, like him. In the cinema of Renoir, when style rules, content will be there to an almost religious degree.

Not that anything in acting should be self-conscious or cute, he believes. It should be all strong and quick. The style accommodates works as superficially different as *Boudu Sauvé des Eaux* (with Michel Simon), *The River* (1950), *Le Carrosse d'Or* (1952), *Le Testament du Dr. Cordelier* (1959), a Jekyll-and-Hyde story with Jean-Louis Barrault, and *Le Déjeuner sur l'Herbe*. In other words, it accommodates neorealism, romantic dialogues with nature, dramas of high and sometimes self-mocking artifice, melodrama, and those peculiarly Renoir moments when comedy dissolves into emotion. He rehearses his actors so that they can quit mannerism and use force instead. We watch them having something unknown to them drawn from their inner resources, as if Renoir had found ideas in their heads which first appeared as little pieces of thread, and then as lengths of string, and then as ropes. Renoir's films are so gentle-spirited that it is easy to miss his innately theatrical instinct for finding the moment when a character is at the end of his tether.

Pagan:
Le Déjeuner sur l'Herbe (1959)

IN LE DÉJEUNER SUR L'HERBE Renoir makes use of an earnestness about topics which is to be found in TV specials. The topics here are artificial insemination and the Common Market. A Professor Alexis is solemnly researching artificial insemination. He is candidate for the Presidency of a united Europe, and related, luckily, to the major chemical fortunes of both France and Germany. At the same time, he is in the middle of announcing his engagement to a beautiful German cousin who loves Scouting. A stuffy engagement ceremony for the press takes place in Renoir's loved Provence and would despoil the countryside except for nature's protest, in the form of a windstorm that sows confusion. Things begin to become bacchanalian in the drowsy heat. The sedate professor is entranced by the sight of a girl bathing naked. Theories about artificial insemination will have to wait till tomorrow. We are once more in the midst of a way of life that flows like a tide.

Renoir is drawn again and again to the polytheistic and materialist conception of nature which has been so ravaged by Christian rationalism. In a pinch, Renoir would trust the pagan view every time; and this great experimenter and ally of novelty is forever looking for the pagan virtues in new forms, believing that it is better to make bad films, always attempting fresh things, than to keep to the tried and already successful. His people expose their spirits to us. Just as his great father loved women for baring their bodies, Jean Renoir loves his characters for the immodesty of baring their souls.

Pax:
Le Caporal Épinglé (1962)

WHERE THE CONVENTIONAL antiwar film piously says that killing people is wrong, Renoir's *Le Caporal Épinglé* gently makes the incontrovertible remark that killing *me* is wrong. The picture is rather like Joseph Heller's savage satirical novel *Catch 22*, in which all the hero's rage and cunning are directed against the people who are trying to prevent his staying alive, most of whom are on his own side. War-film makers are often behind the mood of their period: it has taken a long time for anyone to see the heroic comic possibilities of this kind of softly stated and entirely congenial self-interest.

Like *La Grande Illusion*, *Le Caporal Épinglé* is set in a prison camp. The hero's driving force is simply that he wants to get out of it. Now and again there are scraps of newsreel about the atrocities that are happening in the world beyond, but they haven't very much to do with the reality of his own life. All that he knows is that he is young, and intent on existing if possible; and the enemy guards seem to be in much the same mood. The most obvious advantage possessed by the Germans in this film is that they have first call on the *pissoir*. The prisoners spend a lot of time emptying the cesspool, and the impulse that makes one of them disappear to add to it in the interests of making the job more his own is a comically dignified comment on the pride of working for oneself. This is a sage and touching film. There is a moment of typical compassion when the corporal, beautifully played by Jean-Pierre Cassel, is given a bowl of beans by a friend after his umpteenth escape and a spell in solitary: all he can say, weeping, is that the beans are too hot. Renoir somehow communicates that his comic hero is a man of great virtue, by which he means nothing at all to do with the qualities taught by War Offices or Pentagons.

The soldier's code, he implies, is a counterfeit; togetherness under the flag cannot console anyone for killing or being killed. *Le Caporal Épinglé* takes for granted the fundamental truth, ignored by most people who make battle films, that the catastrophes of war do not happen to men in platoons, they happen to a man in isolation. Renoir's films always express the belief that people's endeavors are admirable whether they come to nought, as they do in *Le Caporal Épinglé*, in which the heroes do the most low-down jobs ("To think we set out to liberate Poland!" says one P.O.W. on sewage duty to another as they clean out cisterns while maintaining an air of unquenched lyric patriotism, overlaid with considerable affront), or whether the characters are engaged in the French Revolution, as in *La Marseillaise*, and changing the whole course of human affairs.

Renoir has always been exhilarated by keen-eyed, strolling characters who are not overbusy with acquitting themselves well. He thinks the Garden of Eden must have had a population of nonheroes and loiterers. For him, heroism lies in having new ideas and in pursuing them alone. Ballochet (Claude Rich), in *Le Caporal Épinglé*, an ex-employee of a gas company who is appointed an interpreter for his fellow prisoners, though he doesn't speak a word of German, disappoints his friend the Corporal—who is never

even allowed the dignity of a Christian name—by refusing
to go on taking part in the Corporal's continuing attempts at
escape, which are all failures until the sixth. Ballochet ac-
cepts the confines of prison camp almost in a mood of
idealism. This is at least better than his old job, which was a
nullity in the prewar order of Christian and chivalrous
tenets: nothing very Christian or chivalrous about the gas
company. To the Corporal's disgust, Ballochet enjoys his
retreat into a liberty of the mind, though he says mildly that
it's annoying to be a loser, and that it plays hell with one's
habits. He seems at first a cowering soul. But not to Renoir,
who shows him at last slowly inspired to walk out of their
prison hut toward the barbed wire, armed with a pair of
pliers from his old days with the gas company. He dies. The
Corporal, the discouraged friend who felt a whiff of contempt that Ballochet had given up trying to escape with him,
is suddenly Ballochet's intimate again, in a shot on Jean-
Pierre Cassel in which he visibly walks every step with the
loner and jumps like a pheasant during a shoot when the
machine guns burst out. Others wanted to take the impossible risk, too, but Ballochet said, "My kind has to go it alone,"
walking away from the others and adjusting his spectacles.
Dignity makes caste disappear. The Corporal is
pinned—*épinglé*—into a system of automatized heroism,
whereas Ballochet was able to see that the prisoners hardly
knew any longer why they were attempting to escape. Still,
the Corporal keeps trying. For Renoir's Corporal, as for an
E. M. Forster character, heroism rests in behaving a little
better in crisis than one normally would.

Eventually the Corporal succeeds in escaping, and
makes his way to Paris with his second-best friend, Pater
(Claude Brasseur). There are meaningless swift goodbyes

and empty promises to meet again at the front: awful to hear social fibs at this stage between two close members of a group that once said gaily, in the early days, that Roosevelt was writing to Hitler, "Dear Adolf, Release French prisoners or we'll declare war," and that made undying promises to have dinner together in Paris when it was all over. Life is full of brief shafts of disappointment. We know that Pater's and the Corporal's vows will never be kept. This is not where their heroism lies. With the completed escape, the Corporal has laid himself open to the arrows of real life's distress, and can find encouragement only in the memory of a German girl, a dentist's assistant, who said, "I like a man who's not a slave."

But the film says at the end that "this is only a beginning"—the idea that was to become the slogan of the student rebels during the uprising of May, 1968. Renoir is the youngest of us, the most gently rebellious, the most studious. Things are never more than a beginning for him. How like him not to have hesitated to make a picture about prisoners of war a quarter of a century after he directed *La Grande Illusion* on the same theme. The later film is not a masterwork, but it moves on the same hawser of sociability in impossible circumstances. An aged and very drunk German whom the escapers meet on a train says to the Corporal and Pater that he likes the French, and he tries to stop Nazi soldiers from catching them. Then he is killed by the Allies in an air attack. As the Corporal and Pater get near the border, they meet an amiable French farmer who turns out to be a First World War prisoner who later married the German woman with whom he had been billeted. A sense of the general flux of things suffuses Renoir's work. There are scenes in *Le Caporal Épinglé* in which the camera abruptly pulls back, as if to "resituate the characters in a better life," as Renoir once put it. The movie is made in revolt against the ruling absurdity of existence, what with the drunk on the train, and the chaotic air attack. The meditative film is watching, with cool eyes, a case of delirium taking place before a softer morning. The delirium is entirely recognizable but entirely unfamiliar, as Renoir would want. His passion for novelty and his breadth of spirit are at the root of his vivacity. He is our perpetual revolutionary and our perpetual beginner.

The Compère of the Game:
Le Petit Théâtre de Jean Renoir
(1969)

LE PETIT THÉÂTRE DE JEAN RENOIR, directed when he
was seventy-five, has the vigor of a first work. It has a modest
appearance, like everything else he has ever done. In form, it
is a series of three sketches that begin on a red-swagged toy
stage. The great director, looking pale but always himself,
behaves as a sort of compère. The picture written by him was
made for television, but it suits the movie screen much
better. The convivial, saddened, magically revived temperament of the last story has some of the nature of *La Règle du
Jeu.*

    Henri Langlois, the archivist who is world film history's
sage, Cerberus, spy, Foreign Legionnaire, and acknow-
ledged king—the scholar of silent movies who calls the
talkies "the babble-toy"; the big witty man whose arms fall
forward as if he would prefer to be on all fours when he is
speaking—opened a season in America of great films from
the Cinémathèque Française archives with Renoir's *Le Petit
Théâtre.* Otherwise it is a season of brilliance, quixotry, love,
and disorder. ("Disorder is the Greek thing. . . . Disorder is
the energy," Langlois said in a hurry at the opening, off-
handedly defending a lifetime.) It is his witness in America
of an aim realized after ages of scholars' squabbles; his

conspiratorial gift to the movie land that has precious little concrete recall of world movies. Typically, the Dionysian antiquarian began the season with this Apollonian film of Renoir's. The picture was made for French and Italian television. That should put no one off, least of all distributors. At seventy-five, the master does things in this film that are as funny, convivial, and moving as anything in his career.

In the middle of the picture, at the end of the second of three sketches, Renoir makes one of his appearances and says, "I invite you now to an evocation of what it is convenient to call the *'belle époque.'* " He looks rather serious. "I know very well," he says, "that the *belle époque* wasn't as beautiful as all that, that it had its injustices, its cruelties, but I like it, because it furnished us with touching elements for the mounting of spectacles." Your head hums a bit with boredom, but this is Renoir, after all. You make room. He goes on, "I asked Jeanne Moreau to be our guide on this excursion into the past. With infinite grace, she agreed to lend her beauty and her talent." It is rather stuffy, like the opening of a fête. Then Jeanne Moreau comes on in a wasp-waisted dress and sings a terrific piece of nineteenth-century sentiment composed by Octave Crémieux and called "When Love Dies." (Marlene Dietrich sang it in *Morocco*.) The solemnity is immense. Love dies splendiferously. The camera moves slowly in and out with heavy respect, like an intimidated member of the chorus tiptoeing around the stage deathbed of a soprano who is elocuting some very long and effulgent last words. So this isn't nostalgia at all. It is high, stone-faced, crackup spoof. The magnetic thing is that Jeanne Moreau's expressions are completely out of sync with the stuff she is singing. In full flood, she looks obscurely distracted. As she belts out a particularly hefty line of lament, a wisp of anxiety will cross her face. Something is bothering her. The song, presumably. Then she will muster herself and carry straight on, gazing at a point that exquisitely just misses the camera, her beautiful eyes sometimes slightly crossed. The famous mouth drags down in misery, and the upper lip gets very long, like someone suppressing a yawn.

The number is simple and mysteriously hilarious. Jeanne Moreau must be very bright. Perhaps funniness often occurs when everything is in good order except for one small thing that has slipped. In this two-minute set piece, it is the visibly skeptical cast of the singer's mind that throws everything out. In the sketch that this squib of a song follows, called "The Electric Waxing Machine," it is something else. Renoir introduces the sketch as an opera: "Well, at least, there are songs, choruses commenting on the action, et cetera, et cetera. It is also very topical, because it is about the struggle between mankind and the machine." A prim and pretty housewife (Marguérite Cassan, superb), a Dresden-faced chirper who is obsessed with cleaning, comes back to her apartment one day and slips dreamily into snowshoe-size carpet slippers before breasting around her living-room floor so as to polish the parquet. Her passion to own an electric floor-waxer easily dwarfs any passion she has ever had for her husband (Pierre Olaf), a benign, decorous man who looks much in need of exhilaration. He has just been upped to second clerk, but his wife pays him no heed at all, apart from saying that the promotion will pay for a polisher. When the man tries to be master in his own house, it is an act that he can sustain only by stalking away from her and delivering experimental pieces of firmness from hid-

den positions in other rooms. He is beaten, of course. The
electric polisher comes to stay. The husband soon dies of a
blow on the head, flat on his back after slipping on the glassy
floor. Sorrowing but practical, the widow quickly gets married again and goes on adoring her floor. "A spot!" she
hisses, on hands and knees, thrilled, while her new man is
trying in his turn to be forceful about getting her not to use
the noisy machine when he is at home. She turns girlish.
"I'm going back to my mother," she whines. The comic bit of
displacement here is that the actress really looks twenty
years too old for the line. The little fable is always perfectly
acted, with funny spurts of fury and some moments of Tati
automation behavior. It also has the unusual and transforming provision that it is cryptically interrupted now and then
by singers, who elbow their way to the camera and wail
rather bossy comments on the action. Joseph Kosma's witty
music—he wrote the score for Renoir's *La Grande Illusion*—is
in the style of, say, the Nadia Boulanger school. It is advanced. The singers look concentrated and forbidding. A
fierce egotism visibly operates among them: a man and a
woman will bawl nastily in counterpoint at each other, for
instance, while a taller man in the middle, irritably holding
another nontune, cranes over them and fixes the camera
with a chill stare. Sometimes a lot of the singers will be
clumped together, desperately pretending to be ordinary
people in the middle of their recondite yelling. There is one
difficult song when they mill, trying vainly to look as if they
were chatting, each of them equipped, for no credible
reason, with a long loaf of bread. Like a Greek chorus, they
have reactions that are a mixture of the high-flown and the
fusspot, and they exclaim a great deal about rapture and
delicious excess in a rather nagging, petit-bourgeois tone of

voice. The little story is gracefully characterized in the performances and very funny about twentieth-century music and ancient Greeks.

The film begins low, with a tale called "The Last Christmas Eve," derived from Hans Christian Andersen. A navy-blue-cheeked tramp has been hired to look hungry outside the window of a restaurant so as to sharpen the Christmas appetites of the gossipy celebrators within, who have the attention span of gnats. The sentimentality of the tramp's last Christmas Eve, spent with an old beggar-woman friend and going to sleep hungry in a snowfall, is not Renoir's, but the talk of the well-heeled, scatty people inside the restaurant is his own and funnily inane. Fighting off thickets of paper streamers, they utter the blithe bird cries of a holiday without a context. ("I *adore* convention," says one man, drumming up enthusiasm for the boring with no visible luck, while everybody else in the room ignores him anyway.) Someone idly recommends whiskey and cayenne for toothache to a wretched beauty who looks as if she has been forced into her tight dress with a monkey wrench. She says little and nurses a painful wisdom tooth. Apart from poverty, though, and the conceits of fairy tales, why does the tramp take on the fanciful job? To assassinate boredom, he seems to suggest. "Hunger, cold, I can manage all those. But boredom . . ." he says faintly. This is a slight piece, made charming and idiosyncratic by Renoir.

The third piece, "The King of Yvetot," is fine enough and characteristic enough to remind you often of Renoir's *La Règle du Jeu.* ("I enjoy repeating myself," Renoir said happily a while ago. "One gets interested.") A character called Duvallier (Fernand Sardou), a heavy, poetic, shambling figure a little like the Octave whom Renoir himself

played in *La Règle du Jeu*, is married to a pretty girl much
younger than he is. They live in the country, in a small town
where the men play bowls and Duvallier always wins. This
nourishes the old French superstition that winners at games
must be in the midst of being cuckolded. He laughs amiably
at that, and continues to dote on his wife. He also deals
sweetly with their maid, who wants to quit service and become a high-class concubine, like Camille or Messalina—"a
hetaera." (She wants to do a lot of things. Later on, she
aspires desperately to own a butcher's shop. "It's perfectly
possible to be a hetaera *and* a butcher," her master says
encouragingly.)

"I'm nervous," says his wife, out of the blue. Why? She
doesn't know. Her skin is tingling and she looks ready to
run. His big head hangs. He's old and she's young, and that's
the root of it—they should separate, he says lugubriously.
No, she says, believing she means it; she is married to a big
bear at loose and alone in the world, and she loves him, and
life without him would be insupportable. In the middle of
this—events in Renoir's best films flow in and out of one
another like water, with unrelated small mishaps interrupt-
ing moments when the people talking are trying to confront
their lives—their dachshund is hurt. The vet comes, in a
very small white car, heralded by the ceremonial but clipped
entrance music of four bars from Beethoven's Fifth. The
crisis passes, the couple and the vet have lunch, the distraught maid produces an uncooked fish, and the vet and
Duvallier strike up an alliance because they discover that
they both believe in loafing. (Duvallier sings a scrap of a
nineteenth-century jingle about the endearing king of
Yvetot, "little known in history," who lay about in bed most
of the time "and slept wonderfully, though without glory.")

The vet falls for the wife, of course. There is a moment when he kisses first the dachshund's head and then the girl's mouth. She looks mildly dissident. Duvallier finds out about the affair very soon. You see his back view going down a lane: an ambling creature, quizzical, much wounded, with a jacket that hangs loose behind. What would the other men in the village do if their wives took lovers? He asks a sailor. "I wouldn't bother myself about it much," says the sailor, and then, with an unmarked turn in the line that is typical of Renoir's dialogue style, "I haven't got a wife." Another adviser says, "I'd kill her, and him, too." "You love her that much?" says Duvallier. "It's not how much I love her," the adviser, who deals in rabbit skins, says loftily, "but I wouldn't want to be taken for a fool." The wife blooms in love; the aging husband, hanging his heavy head like a cart horse put out to grass and stumbling away into the world beyond his once idyllic garden to think, is smartly saluted by a tramp. The locals admire his luck at bowls but take it for granted that it means he is unlucky in love. On the way to join them, he picks a straw of grass, wipes the tears from his papery cheeks, and gives some money to the saluting bum, whose experience of love and sex turns out to be slight when Duvallier asks for advice. "Your orders are to get plastered," Duvallier says gently. "Aye, aye, sir," says the tramp, this unmarried innocent, touched for no reason he can put his finger on. "What would you do if your wife cheated?" Duvallier asks another man near the village. "She's too old" is the reply.

Duvallier himself is irretrievably pacific, but he comports himself like no fool. The vet, in an immolatory mood masked as belligerence, offers pistols. No taker. "You don't wish to duel with me?" says the vet piteously. I don't think so,

Duvallier holds. A possible course, and better, would be to
live out the triangle as it is. "But there are conventions," says
the vet, scandalized. None of this is Duvallier's style, which is
the style of reconciling. He is old, if hurt. His wife is
young, if casual; she's fond of him. And the vet can't imagine
life without either of them, he says, telling the patent truth.
Duvallier typically regards it as his task to cheer everyone
up. The distraught vet talks of going to China. Think of my
wife, says Duvallier with his usual *douceur* of spirit. But it
would be a revolution to stay together, all of us, says the
vet. On the contrary, says Duvallier, it is the small revolutions that make life bearable. The vet beams. Duvallier goes
on: about revolutions in the kitchen, the bedroom, the village square, which he considerably dreads because he is
going to be laughed at. "You're an extraordinary man," says
the vet.

　　And then, at this rather sad moment in praise of ac-
commodation, Renoir suddenly seizes the last few seconds
of the picture and throws them into the air like a kite,
turning a shot of people playing bowls and laughing at the
cuckolded Duvallier into an image of the husband, wife, and
lover laughing together, and then, pulling back in a con-
tinuous shot, into the sight of them still laughing together
but now as actors taking their curtain call. The speed is
beautiful. This is a little work by a great master, and it is little
partly because he can do what he wants in the breath of a
second. That may have something to do with the succinct-
ness of age, but it also has something to do with his lifelong
genius for throwing great things away very fast. The last
part of the film, which is spiked with marvellous funniness
and spirit, embodies some rather serious ideas about the
tolerance of contradictions—a notion that runs through

Renoir's work—but he gives us the whole piece as a toy, for the fun of it. He would never have enjoyed being a general, which is the way a good many directors see their role. He is a born corporal, teaching a platoon how to hang on to a horse, because that's the entertaining part. There are a lot of moments in the picture that one wishes would go on longer, but he cuts them short out of a sure instinct that there are plenty more where these came from. The prodigality makes your eyes sting, and not because of his age.

BOUDU SAUVÉ DES EAUX (1932)
(The Museum of Modern Art
Film Still Archive)

TONI (1934)
(Contemporary Films/
McGraw-Hill)

LE CRIME DE MONSIEUR LANGE (1935)
(The Museum of Modern Art
Film Still Archive)

LES BAS-FONDS (1936)
(The Museum of Modern Art
Film Still Archive)

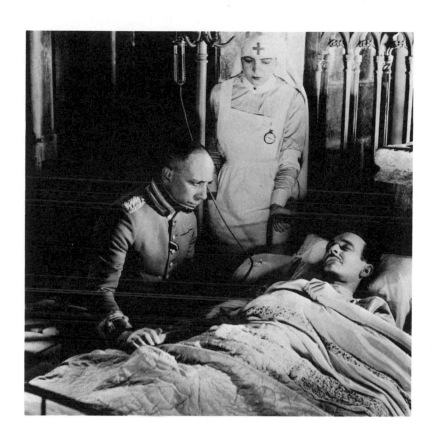

LA GRANDE ILLUSION
(1936-37)
(Janus)

LA GRANDE ILLUSION
(1936-37)
(Janus)

LA GRANDE ILLUSION
(1936-37)
(Janus)

LA MARSEILLAISE (1937)
(Contemporary Films/
McGraw-Hill)

LA RÈGLE DU JEU
(1939)
(Janus)

LA RÈGLE DU JEU
(1939)
(Janus)

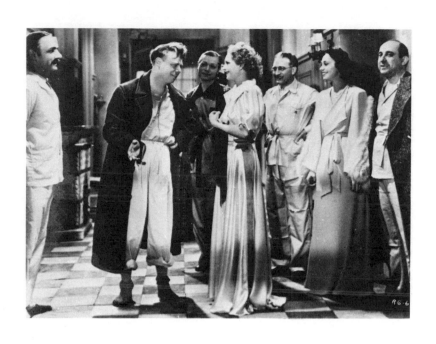

LA RÈGLE DU JEU
(1939)
(Janus)

LA RÈGLE DU JEU
(1939)
(Janus)

ELÉNA ET LES HOMMES (1956)
(The Museum of Modern Art
Film Still Archive)

LE DÉJEUNER SUR L'HERBE (1959)
(Contemporary Films/
McGraw-Hill)

LE CAPORAL ÉPINGLÉ (1961-62)
(Contemporary Films/
McGraw-Hill)

LE PETIT THÉÂTRE DE JEAN RENOIR
(1969)
(Phoenix Films)

Filmography

UNE VIE SANS JOIE, made in 1924 (reedited in 1927 and released as *CATHERINE*).
80 minutes

Directed by Albert Dieudonné
Screenplay by Jean Renoir from a story by Jean Renoir and
  Pierre Lestringuez
Produced by Jean Renoir
Photographed by Jean Bachelet and Gibory

CAST:

Catherine Hessling *as Catherine Ferand*
Albert Dieudonné *as M. Mallet, the owner*
Pierre Philippe *as Adolph, the pimp*
Pierre Champagne *as the younger Mallet*
Oléo *as a prostitute*
Georges Térof *as Gédéon Grané*
Eugénie Naud *as Madame Laisné*
Jean Renoir *as the subprefect*
Louis Gauthier *as Georges Mallet*

LA FILLE DE L'EAU, made in 1924 (English-language title
  THE WHIRLPOOL OF FATE).
70 minutes

Directed by Jean Renoir
Screenplay by Pierre Lestringuez

Produced by Jean Renoir
Photographed by Jean Bachelet and Gibory
Assistant director Pierre Champagne
Sets conceived by Jean Renoir

CAST:

Catherine Hessling *as Virginia Rosaert*
Pierre Phillippe *as Uncle Jef*
Pierre Champagne *as Justin Crepoix*
Harold Lewingston *as Georges Raynal*
Maurice Touzé *as the little vagabond*
Georges Térof *as M. Raynal*
Henriette Moret *as La Roussette*
Charlotte Clasis *as Mme. Raynal*
Pierre Renoir *as a peasant*
André Derain *as the owner of "Au Bon Coin"*
Van Doren *as the leading man*

NANA, made in 1925-26.
98 minutes

Directed by Jean Renoir
Screenplay by Pierre Lestringuez (based on Émile Zola's
    novel), adapted by Jean Renoir; titles by Denise
    Leblond-Zola
Produced by Jean Renoir
Photographed by Jean Bachelet and Edmund Corwin
Assistant director André Cerf
Edited by Jean Renoir

CAST:

Catherine Hessling *as Nana*
Werner Krauss *as Count Muffat*

Jacqueline Forzane *as Countess Sabine Muffat*
Jean Angelo *as Count de Vandeuvres*
Raymond Guérin-Catelain *as Georges Hugon*
Pierre Champagne *as La Falaise*
Pierre Philippe *as Bordenave*
Valeska Gert *as Zoé, Nana's maid*
Harbacher *as Francis, Nana's hairdresser*
André Cerf *as Le Tigre, Nana's groom*
Claude Moore *as Fauchery*
Jacqueline Ford *as Rose Mignon*
Nita Romani *as Satin*
Marie Prévost *as Gago*
René Koval *as Fontan*
Pierre Braunberger ⎱ *spectators at Le Théâtre des*
R. Turgy ⎰ *Variétés*

SUR UN AIR DE CHARLESTON, made in 1926 (alternate title *CHARLESTON-PARADE*).
22 minutes

Directed by Jean Renoir
Screenplay by Pierre Lestringuez from an idea by André Cerf
Assistant director André Cerf
Photographed by Jean Bachelet
Music by Clément Doucet

CAST:
Catherine Hessling *as the dancer*
Johnny Hugging *as the explorer*
Pierre Braunberger ⎱ *as angels*
Pierre Lestringuez ⎰

LA P'TITE LILI, made in 1926.

11 minutes

Directed by Alberto Cavalcanti
Screenplay by Alberto Cavalcanti from a song by Louis
     Benech
Produced by Pierre Braunburger
Photography by Rogers
Edited by Marguerite Renoir
Music by Max de La Sasinière
Sets by Eric Aës

CAST:

Catherine Hessling *as La P'tite Lili*
Jean Renoir *as the pimp*
Guy Ferrand *as the singer*
Roland Caillaux *as the concierge*
Eric Aës ⎫
Rogers   ⎬ *silhouettes*
Dido Freire ⎭

MARQUITA, made in 1926-27 (originally titled
     MARCHETA, from a song by Saint Granier).

87 minutes

Directed by Jean Renoir
Screenplay by Pierre Lestringuez from an adaption by Jean
     Renoir
Produced by Artistes Réunis
Photographed by Jean Bachelet and Raymond Agnel

Assistant director M. Gargour
Sets by Robert-Jules Garnier

CAST:

Jean Angelo *as Prince Vlasco*
Marie-Louise Iribe *as Marquita*
Henri Debain *as Count Dimitrieff*
Lucien Mancini *as the stepfather*
Pierre Philippe *as the casino owner*
Pierre Champagne *as a taxi driver*

LA PETITE MARCHANDE D'ALLUMETTES, made in 1926 (English-language title *THE LITTLE MATCII GIRL*).

29 minutes

Directed by Jean Renoir collaborating with Jean Tedesco
Screenplay by Jean Renoir from the Hans Christian Andersen story
Produced by Jean Renoir and Jean Tedesco
Photographed by Jean Bachelet
Assistant directors Claude Heyman and Simone Hamiguet
Music from Mendelssohn, Strauss, Wagner, and others

CAST:

Catherine Hessling *as the little match girl*
Jean Storm *as the young man and the soldier*
Manuel Raaby *as the policeman and the emissary of death*
Amy Wells *as the dancing doll*

TIRE AU FLANC, made in 1928 (*THE SLACKER*).

80 minutes

Directed by Jean Renoir
Screenplay by Jean Renoir, Claude Heymenn, and André
    Cerf from a play by A. Mouézy-Eon and A. Sylvane
Produced by Pierre Braunberger
Photographed by Jean Bachelet
Assistant directors André Cerf and Lola Markovitch
Titles and drawings by André Rigaud
Sets by Eric Aës

CAST:

Georges Pomiès *as Jean Dubois d'Ombelles*
Michel Simon *as Joseph*
Felix Oudart *as Colonel Brochard*
Jeanne Hibling *as Solange Standin*
Jean Storm *as Lieutenant Daumel*
Paul Velsa *as Corporal Bourrache*
Manuel Raaby *as the adjutant*
Fridette Fatton *as Georgette*
Maryanne *as Mme. Blandin*
Zellas *as Muflot*
Kinny Dorlay *as Lily, Solange's sister*
Esther Kiss *as Mme. Flechais*
André Cerf ⎱ *soldiers*
Max Dalban ⎰

LE TOURNOI DANS LA CITÉ, made in 1928.

72 minutes

Directed by Jean Renoir
Screenplay by Henri Dupuy-Mazuel and André Jaeger-
    Schmidt; adapted by Jean Renoir

Produced by Maroussem and François Harispuru
Photographed by Marcel Lucien and Maurice Desfassiaux
Assistant director André Cerf
Edited by André Cerf
Sets by Robert Mallet-Stevens

CAST:

Aldo Nadi *as François de Baynes*
Jackie Monnier *as Isabelle Ginori*
Enrique Rivero *as Henri de Rogier*
Manuel Raaby *as Catherine de Médicis*
Suzanne Despres *as Countess Baynes*
Gérard Mock *as Charles IX*
Vivian Clarens *as Lucrèce Pazzi*
Narval *as Antonio*
Janvier *as the King's Guard officer*
William Aguet *as Master of the Horse*
Max Dalban *as Captain of the Watch*

LE BLED, made in 1929 (*THE BACK OF BEYOND*).
87 minutes

Directed by Jean Renoir
Screenplay by Henri Dupuy-Mazuel and André Jaeger-
    Schmidt; adapted by Jean Renoir; titles by André
    Giraud
Produced by Henri Dupuy-Mazuel
Photographed by Marcel Lucien and Morizet
Assistant directors André Cerf and René Arcy-Hennery
Edited by Marguerite Renoir
Sets by William Aguet

CAST:

Jackie Monnier *as Claude Duvernet*
Enrique Rivero *as Pierre Hoffer*
Arquillière *as Christian Hoffer*
Diana Hart *as Diane Duvernet*
Manuel Raaby *as Manuel Duvernet*
Bérardi Aissa *as Zoubir*
Jacques Becker *as a farm laborer*
Hadj Ben Yasmina *as the chauffeur*
M. Martin *as the falconer Ahmed*
Mme. Rozier *as Marie-Jeanne*

LE PETIT CHAPERON ROUGE, made in 1929.
Short film

Directed by Alberto Cavalcanti and Jean Renoir
Screenplay by Alberto Cavalcanti and Jean Renoir; adapted
    from a story by Charles Perrault
Produced by M. Guillaume
Photographed by Marcel Lucien
Edited by Marguerite Renoir
Music by Maurice Jaubert

CAST:

Catherine Hessling *as Little Red Riding Hood*
Jean Renoir *as the wolf*
André Cerf *as the notary*
Pierre Prévert *as a girl*
Pablo Quevedo *as the young man*
La Montagne *as a farmer*
William Aguet *as an old Englishwoman*

LA CHASSE À LA FORTUNE, made in 1929-30 (alternate
   title *LA CHASSE AU BONHEUR*).

Short film

Directed by Rochus Gliese
Screenplay by Lotte Reiniger and Carl Koch, from an idea
   by Alex Trasser
Produced by Comenius Films
Photographed by Fritz Arno Wagner
Music by Theo Mackenben

CAST:

Jean Renoir *as a businessman*
Catherine Hessling *as Fortune*
Bertold Bartosche *as the pedlar*
Jean Tedesco ⎫
Alexander Murski ⎬ *silhouettes*
Amy Wells ⎭

ON PURGE BÉBÉ, made in 1931.

62 minutes

Directed by Jean Renoir; this was Renoir's first 100% talking
   film
Screenplay by Jean Renoir from the Georges Feydeau play
Produced by Charles David
Photographed by Théodore Sparkuhl and Roger Hubert
Assistant directors Claude Heymann and Pierre Schwab
Edited by Jean Mamy
Sets by Gabriel Scongnamillo

CAST:

Michel Simon *as Chouilloux*
Marguerita Pierry *as Julie Follavoine*
Olga Valery *as Clémence Chouilloux*
Louvigny *as Follavoine*
Sacha Tarride *as Toto*
Nicole Fernandez *as Rose*
Fernandel *as Truchet*

LA CHIENNE, made in 1931.

100 minutes

Directed by Jean Renoir
Screenplay by Jean Renoir and André Girard from the
      Georges de la Fouchardière novel
Produced by Charles David and Roger Woog
Photographed by Théodore Sparkuhl and Roger Hubert
Assistant directors Claude Heymann and Pierre Prévert
Edited by Denise Batcheff-Tual, Marguerite Renoir, and
      Jean Renoir
Music by Eugénie Buffet
Sets by Gabriel Scongnamillo

CAST:

Michel Simon *as Maurice Legrand*
Madeline Bérubet *as Adèle Legrand*
Janie Marèze *as Lulu Pelletier*
Georges Flammand *as André Jauguin, called Dédé*
Gaillard *as Sergeant Alexis Godard*
Jean Gehret *as Dagòdet*

Lucien Mancini *as Wallstein, the gallery owner*
Sylvain Itkine *as the lawyer*
Alexandre Rignault *as Langelard, the art critic*
Max Dalban *as Bonnard*
Colette Borelli *as Lily, Lulu's friend*
Romain Bouquet *as M. Henriot, store owner*
Pierre Destys *as Gustave*
Jane Pierson *as the concierge*
Henri Guisol *as Amédée, a waiter*
Argentin *as the magistrate*
Mlle. Doryans *as Yvonne*

LA NUIT DU CARREFOUR, made in 1932.

80 minutes

Directed by Jean Renoir
Screenplay by Jean Renoir and Georges Simenon from a
    Georges Simenon novel
Produced by Jacques Becker
Photographed by Marcel Lucien and Asselin
Assistant directors Jacques Becker and Maurice Blondeau
Edited by Marguerite Renoir, assisted by Suzanne Troye
    and Walter Ruttmann
Sets by William Aguet, assisted by Jean Castanier

CAST:

Pierre Renoir *as Inspector Maigret*
Georges Térof *as Lucas*
Winna Winifred *as Elsa Andersen*
Georges Koudria *as Carl Andersen*
Dignimont *as Oscar*

Lucie Vallat *as Oscar's wife*
G. A. Martin *as Grandjean*
Jean Gehret *as Emile Michonnet*
Michel Duran *as Jojo, the garage attendant*
Jean Mitray *as Arsène*
Max Dalban *as the doctor*
Gaillard *as the butcher*
Jeanne Pierson *as Mme. Michonnet*
Boulicot *as a policeman*
Manuel Raaby *as Guido*

CHOTARD & CIE, made in 1932.
113 minutes

Directed by Jean Renoir
Screenplay by Jean Renoir and Roger Ferdinand from the
     play by Roger Ferdinand
Produced by Roger Ferdinand
Photographed by Mundwiller
Assistant director Jacques Becker
Edited by Marguerite Renoir and Suzanne de Troye
Sets by Jean Castanier

CAST:

Fernand Charpin *as François Chotard*
Jeanne Lory *as Marie, his wife*
Georges Pomiès *as Julien Collinet*
Jeanne Boitel *as Reine, his wife*
Malou Treki *as Augustine*
Louis Tunk *as the subprefect*

Dignimont *as Parpaillon, Julien's friend*
Max Dalban *as a grocery shop assistant*
Robert Seller *as the police chief*
Fabien Loris *as a guest at the ball*

BOUDU SAUVÉ DES EAUX, made in 1932.
83 minutes

Directed by Jean Renoir
Screenplay by Jean Renoir and Albert Valentin from the
    René Fauchois play
Produced by Michel Simon and Jean Gehret
Photographed by Marcel Lucien and Asselin
Assistant directors Jacques Becker and Georges Darnoux
Edited by Marguerite Renoir and Suzanne de Troye
Music by Raphael and Johann Strauss
Sets by Jean Castanier and Laurent

CAST:

Michel Simon *as Boudu*
Charles Granval *as Lestingois*
Marcel Haina *as his wife*
Séverine Lerczinska *as Anne-Marie*
Jean Dasté *as the student*
Max Dalban *as Godin*
Jean Gehret *as Vigour*
Jacques Becker *as the poet*
Jane Pierson *as Rose, a maid*
Georges Darnoux *as a guest*

MADAME BOVARY, made in 1933.
102 minutes (210-minute version never shown)

Directed by Jean Renoir
Screenplay by Jean Renoir from Gustave Flaubert's novel
Produced by Gaston Gallimard
Photographed by Jean Bachelet and Gibory
Assistant directors Jacques Becker and Pierre Desouches
Edited by Marguerite Renoir
Music by Darius Milhaud and Donizetti
Sets by Robert Gys
Costumes by Medgyes

CAST:

Valentine Tessier *as Emma, Madame Bovary*
Pierre Renoir *as Charles Bovary*
Daniel Lecourtois *as Léon*
Fernand Fabre *as Rodolphe*
Alice Tissot *as Charles Bovary's mother*
Helena Manson *as the first Mme. Bovary*
Pierre Larquey *as Hippolyte*
Max Dearly *as Homais, the pharmacist*
Robert le Vigan *as Lheureux*
Maryanne *as Mme. Homais*
Léon Larive *as the prefect*
Florencie *as Abbe Bournisien*
Romain Bouquet *as Guillaumin, the notary*
Georges Cahuzac *as Rouault*
Allain Dhurtal *as the surgeon*
Henry Vilbert *as Canivet*
Robert Moore *as the footman*
Georges Denebourg *as the Marquis de Vaubyessard*
Edmond Beauchamp *as Binet*

André Fouchet *as Justin, the chemist*
Jean Gehret *as the prefect*
René Bloch *as the coachman*
Marthe Mellot *as the old Nicaise*
Monet Dinay *as Félicité*
Christiane d'Or *as Mme. Lefrançois*

TONI, made in 1934.

90 minutes

Directed by Jean Renoir
Screenplay by Jean Renoir and Carl Einstein, suggested by a
    newspaper article
Produced by Pierre Gaut
Assistant directors Georges Darnoux and Antonio Can
Assistant Luchino Visconti
Edited by Marguerite Renoir and Suzanne de Troye
Music by Paul Bozzi
Sets by Léon Bourelly and Marius Brauquier

CAST:

Charles Blavette *as Toni (Antonio Canova)*
Celian Montalvan *as Josefa*
Jenny Hélia *as Maria*
Max Dalban *as Albert*
Edouard Delmont *as Fernand*
Andrex *as Gaby*
André Kovatchevitch *as Sebastien*
Paul Bozzi *as guitarist Jacques Bozzi*

LE CRIME DE MONSIEUR LANGE, made in 1935.
90 minutes

Directed by Jean Renoir
Screenplay by Jacques Prévert from a story by Jean Renoir
      and Jean Castanier
Produced by André Halley des Fontaines
Photographed by Jean Bachelet
Assistant directors Jacques Prévert and Georges Darnoux
Edited by Marguerite Renoir
Music by Jean Wiener and Joseph Kosma
Sets by Jean Castanier and Robert Gys, assisted by Roger
      Blin

CAST:

René Lefèvre *as Amédé Lange*
Jules Berry *as Batala*
Florelle *as Valentine*
Nadia Sibirskaïa *as Estelle*
Sylvia Bataille *as Edith*
Henri Guisol *as Meunier*
Marcel Levesque *as Bessard, the concierge*
Odette Talazac *as his wife*
Maurice Baquet *as Charles, his son*
Jacques Brunius *as Daigneur*
Sylvain *as Batala's cousin, a retired police inspector*
Edmond Beauchamp *as a priest on the train*
René Genin *as a cafe customer*
Marcel Duhamel ⎫
Jean Dasté   ⎬ *printers*
Guy Decomble   ⎭
Paul Grimault

Paul Demange *as a creditor*
Claire Gérard *as the prostitute*

LA VIE EST À NOUS, made in 1936 (English-language title
       PEOPLE OF FRANCE).
66 minutes

Directed by Jean Renoir with the help of Jacques Becker,
       Jean-Paul Le Chanois, Henri Cartier-Bresson, Pierre
       Unik, B. Brunius, and André Vaillant-Coutourier
Screenplay by Jean Renoir and André Zwoboda
Produced by the Parti Communiste Français
Photographed by Jean Isnard, Jean-Serge Bourgoin,
       Claude Renoir, and Alain Douarinou
Edited by Marguerite Renoir
Music the "Internationale," other songs of the Popular
       Front, Shostakovich
Banned by censors in France and not shown publicly there
       until 1969

CAST:

Jean Dast *as the schoolmaster*
Jacques Brunius *as the president of the Conseil d'Administration*
Max Dalban *as Brochard*
Madeline Solange *as a worker*
Charles Blavette *as Tonin*
Jean Renoir *as the bistro owner*
Edy Debray *as the usher*
Henri Pons *as M. Lecocq*
Gabrielle Fontant *as Mme. Lecocq*

Gaston Modot *as Philippe*
Léon Larive *as a customer at the auction*
Nadia Sibirskaïa *as Ninette*
Marcel Duhamel *as the National Volunteer*
O'Brady *as the car washer*
Julien Bertheau ⎫
Guy Favières   ⎬ *unemployed workers*
Jacques Becker ⎪
Tristan Sevère ⎭
Jean-Paul Le Chanois *as P'tit Louis*
Emile Drain *as Gustave Bertin*
Sylvain Itkine *as the accountant*
Simone Guisin *as a woman at the casino*
Teddy Michaux *as a fascist*
Pierre Unik   ⎫
Madeline Dox   ⎬ *secretaries*
Fernand Bercher ⎭
Claire Gérard *as a woman in the street*
Roger Blin *as a sailor*
Georges Spanelly *as the factory manager*
Marcel Lesieur *as a garage owner*
Charles Charras ⎫
Francis Lemarque ⎬ *singers*

AS THEMSELVES

Marcel Cachin
André Marty
Paul Vaillant-Coutourier
Jean Renaud
Martha Desrumeaux
Marcel Gitton
Jacques Duclos

Maurice Thorez
and the involuntary participation of Colonel de la Rocque

UNE PARTIE DE CAMPAGNE, made in 1936.
37 minutes

Directed by Jean Renoir
Screenplay by Jean Renoir, based on the short story by Guy
    de Maupassant
Produced by Pierre Braunberger
Assistant directors Yves Allegret, Jacques Becker, Jacques
    Brunius, Henri Cartier-Bresson, Luchino Visconti,
    Claude Heymann
Edited by Marguerite Renoir and Marinette Cadix
Music by Joseph Kosma
Sets by Robert Gys

CAST:

Sylvia Bataille *as Henriette Dufour*
Georges Darnoux *as Henri*
Jacques Borel *as Rodolphe*
Jeanne Marken *as Mme. Juliette Dufour*
André Gabriello *as M. Cyprien Dufour*
Paul Temps *as Anatole*
Gabrielle Fontan *as Grandmother Dufour*
Jean Renoir *as Poulain, the innkeeper*
Marguerite Renoir *as the servant*
Pierre Lestringuez *as the curé*
Jacques Becker *as a seminary student*
Alain Renoir *as a little boy*

LES BAS-FONDS, made in 1936.

91 minutes

Directed by Jean Renoir
Screenplay by Jacques Companeez, Eugène Zamatin;
    adapted from the Maxim Gorky play by Charles Spaak,
    Jean Renoir
Produced by Vladimir Zederbaum
Photographed by Jean Bachelet
Assistant directors Jacques Becker, Joseph Soiffer
Edited by Marguerite Renoir
Music by Jean Wiener
Sets by Eugène Lourié, Hughes Laurent
Costumes by Alexander Kamenka

CAST:

Louis Jouvet *as the Baron*
Jean Gabin *as Pepel*
Suzy Prim *as Vasilissa*
Vladamir Sokoloff *as Kostilev*
Junie Astor *as Natacha*
Robert Le Vigan *as the actor*
André Gabriello *as the Inspector*
Camille Bert *as the Count*
Léon Larive *as Felix*
René Génin *as Luka, the drunkard*
Jany Holt *as Nastia, the prostitute*
Maurice Baquet *as Aliochka, the accordionist*
Lucien Mancini *as the restaurant owner*
Paul Temps *as Satine*
Henri Saint-Isles *as Kletsch*
Robert Ozanne *as Jabot*
Nathalie Alexeieff *as Anna*
Jacques Becker *as a silhouette*

LA GRANDE ILLUSION, made in 1936-37.

114 minutes

Directed by Jean Renoir
Screenplay by Charles Spaak, Jean Renoir
Produced by Frank Rollmer, Albert Pinkovitch
Photographed by Christian Matras, with Claude Renoir,
    Bourreud, Jean Bourgoin
Assistant director Jacques Becker
Edited by Marguerite Renoir
Music by Joseph Kosma
Sets by Eugène Lourié

CAST:

Jean Gabin *as Maréchal*
Pierre Fresnay *as de Boïeldieu*
Erich von Stroheim *as von Rauffenstein*
Marcel Dalio *as Rosenthal*
Dita Parlo *as Elsa*
Julien Carette *as the actor*
Gaston Modot *as the engineer*
Jean Dasté *as the teacher*
Georges Paclet *as a French soldier*
Jacques Becker *as an English officer*
Sylvain Itkine *as Demolder*

LA MARSEILLAISE, made in 1937.

135 minutes

Directed by Jean Renoir
Screenplay by Jean Renoir with the help of Carl Koch, and
    M. and Mme. N. Martel-Dreyfus for the historical de-
    tails

Produced for Confédération Générale de Travail
Photographed by Jean Bourgoin, Alain Douarinou, Jean-Marie Maillols, Jean-Paul Alphen, Jean Louis
Assistant directors Jacques Becker, Claude Renoir (nephew of Jean Renoir), Jean-Paul Le Chanois, Claude Renoir (brother of Jean Renoir)
Edited by Marguerite Renoir, Marthe Huguet
Music by Joseph Cosma, Sauveplane, Lalande, Grétry, Rameau, Mozart, Bach, Rouget de Lisle
Sets by Léon Barsacq, Georges Wakhevitch, Jean Perrier
Shadow theater Lotte Reininger

CAST:

The Court
Pierre Renoir *as Louis XVI*
Lise Delamare *as Marie Antoinette*
Léon Larive *as Picard, Louis XVI's valet*
William Aguet *as La Rochefoucauld*
Elisa Ruis *as Mme. de Lamballe*
G. Lefébvre *as Mme. Elizabeth*

The Civil and Military Authorities
Louis Jouvet *as Roederer*
Jean Aquistapace *as the mayor of the village*
Georges Spanally *as La Chesnaye*
Jacque Catelain *as Langlade*
Pierre Nay *as Dubouchange*
Edmond Castel *as Leroux*

The Aristocrats
Aimé Clariond *as Saint-Laurent*
Maurice Escande *as the lord of the villege*
André Zibrol *as M. de Saint-Méry*
Jean Aymé *as M. de Fougerolles*

Irène Joachim *as Mme. de Saint-Laurent*

The Inhabitants of Marseille
Andrex *as Arnaud*
Edmond Ardisson *as Bonnier*
Jean-Louis Allibert *as Moissant*
Jenny Hélia *as the questioner*
Paul Dulac *as Javel*
Ferdinand Flament *as Ardisson*
Georges Péclet *as Lieutenant Pignatel*
Géo Dorlys *as a Marseille Leader*
Géo Lastry *as Captaine Massugue*
Adolphe Autran *as the drummer*
Alex Truchy *as Cuculière*

The People
Nadia Sibirskaïa *as Louison*
Edouard Delmont *as Cabri*
Séverine Lerczinska *as a peasant woman*
Edmond Beauchamp *as the curé*
Gaston Modot ⎫
             ⎬ *volunteers*
Julien Carette ⎭
Marthe Marty *as Bonnier's mother*

LA BÊTE HUMAINE, made in 1938.
105 minutes

Directed by Jean Renoir
Screenplay by Jean Renoir, assisted by Denise Leblond-Zola
    from the Émile Zola novel
Produced by Robert Hakim and Roland Tual
Photographed by Curt Courant and Claude Renoir
Assistant directors Claude Renoir (sen.) and Suzanne de
    Troye

Edited by Marguerite Renoir
Music by Joseph Kosma
Sets by Eugène Lourié

CAST:

Jean Gabin *as Jacques Lantier*
Simone Simon *as Séverine Roubaud*
Fernand Ledoux *as Roubaud*
Julien Carette *as Pecqueux*
Blanchette Brunoy *as Flore*
Gérard Landry *as Dauvergne's son*
Jacques Berlioz *as Grandmorin*
Jean Renoir *as Cabûche*
Marcel Perez *as a railway employee*
Jenny Hélia *as Philomène*
Marceau *as a mechanic*
Tony Corteggiani *as the section boss*
André Tavernier *as the magistrate*
Colette Régis *as Mme. Victoire*
Claire Gérard *as a traveller*
Charlotte Classis *as Phasie Misard*
Georges Spanelly *as Grandmorin's secretary*
Guy Deconble *as a railway crossing guard*
Georges Péclet *as a railway employee*
Émile Gènevois ⎱
Jacques Brunius ⎰ *farmhands*

LA RÈGLE DU JEU, made in 1939.

113 minutes

Directed by Jean Renoir
Screenplay by Jean Renoir, with the collaboration of Carl
    Koch

Produced by Jean Renoir, Claude Renoir
Photographed by Jean Bachelet
Assistant directors André Zwoboda, Henri Cartier-Bresson
Edited by Marguerite Renoir, assisted by Marthe Huguet
Music by Mozart, Monsigny, Saint-Saëns, Johann Strauss,
    arranged by Robert Desormières and Joseph Kosma
Sets by Eugène Lourié, Max Douy
Costumes by Coco Chanel

CAST:

Marcel Dalio *as Robert de la Chesnaye*
Nora Grégor *as Christine de la Chesnaye*
Roland Toutain as *André Jurieu*
Jean Renoir *as Octave*
Mila Parely *as Geneviève de Marrast*
Paulette Dubost *as Lisette*
Gaston Modot *as Schumacher*
Julien Carette *as Marceau*
Pierre Magnier *as the General*
Pierre Nay *as Saint-Aubin*
Richard Francoeur *as La Bruyère*
Eddy Debray *as Corneille, the majordomo*
Léon Larive *as the cook*
Claire Gérard *as Mme. La Bruyère*
Anne Mayan *as Jackie, Christine's niece*
Lise Elina *as the radio reporter*
Tony Corteggiani *as the huntsman*
Camille François *as the radio speaker*
André Zwobada *as the engineer*
Henri Cartier-Bresson *as the English servant*

LA TOSCA, made in 1939.

96 minutes

Directed by Carl Koch, started by Jean Renoir
Screenplay adapted by Jean Renoir, Carl Koch, and
    Luchino Visconti from the play by Victorien Sardou
Produced by Arturo A. Ambrogio
Photographed by Ubaldo Arata
Edited by Gino Bretone
Music by Puccini

CAST:

Imperio Argentina *as Tosca*
Michel Simon *as Scarpia*
Rossano Brazzi *as Mario Cavaradossi*
Massimo Girotti *as Angeloti*

SWAMP WATER, made in 1941.

86 minutes

Directed by Jean Renoir
Screenplay by Dudley Nichols, from the novel by Vereen
    Bell
Produced by Irving Pichel
Photography by Peverell Marley and Lucien Ballard
Edited by Walter Thompson
Music by David Buttolph
Sets by Thomas Little
Costumes by Gwen Wakeling

CAST:

Dana Andrews *as Ben Ragan*
Walter Huston *as Thursday Ragan*

John Carradine *as Jesse Wick*
Eugene Pallette *as Sheriff Jeb MacKane*
Anne Baxter *as Julie Keefer*
Walter Brennan *as Tom Keefer*
Mary Howard *as Hannah Ragan*
Virginia Gilmore *as Mabel McKenzie*
Ward Bond *as Jim Dorson*
Guinn Williams *as Bud Dorson*
Russell Simpson *as Marty McCord*
Joseph Sawyer *as Hardy Ragan*
Paul Burns *as Tulle McKenzie*
Dave Morris *as the barber*
Frank Austin *as Fred Ulm*
Matt Willis *as Miles Tonkin*

THIS LAND IS MINE, made in 1943.
103 minutes

Directed by Jean Renoir
Screenplay by Dudley Nichols and Jean Renoir
Produced by Dudley Nichols and Jean Renoir
Photographed by Frank Redman
Assistant director Edward Donohue
Edited by Frederick Knudston
Music by Lothar Perl
Sets by Darrel Silvera and Al Fclds

CAST:

Charles Laughton *as Albert Mory*
George Sanders *as Georges Lambert*
Maureen O'Hara *as Louise Martin*
Kent Smith *as Paul Martin*

Walter Slezak *as Major von Keller*
Una O'Conner *as Albert Mory's mother*
Phillip Merivale *as Professor Sorel*
Thurston Hall *as Major Henry Manville*
Georges Coulouris *as the prosecutor*
Nancy Gates *as Julie Grant*
Ivan Simpson *as the presiding Judge*
John Donat *as Edmond Lorraine*
Frank Alton *as Lieutenant Schwartz*
Leo Bulgakov *as the little man*
Wheaton Chambors *as Lorraine*
Cecile Weston *as Mrs. Lorraine*

SALUTE TO FRANCE, made in 1944.

20 minutes

Directed by Jean Renoir in collaboration with Garson Kanin
Screenplay by Philippe Dunne, Jean Renoir, and Burgess
    Meredith
Produced by the Office of War Information, New York
Photographed by the Army Pictorial Service
Edited by Helen van Dongen

CAST:

Claude Dauphin *as Jacques, narrator, soldier, and other multiple
    roles*
Burgess Meredith *as Tommy*
Garson Kanin *as Joe*

THE SOUTHERNER, made in 1945 (alternate title *HOLD
    AUTUMN IN YOUR HAND*).
91 minutes

Directed by Jean Renoir
Screenplay by Jean Renoir from the George Sessions Perry
    novel *Hold Autumn in Your Hand*; adapted by Hugo
    Butler
Produced by David L. Loew and Robert Hakim
Photographed by Lucien Andriot
Assistant director Robert Aldrich
Edited by Gregg Tallas
Music by Werner Jannsen
Sets by Eugène Lourié

CAST:

Zachary Scott *as Sam Tucker*
Betty Field *as Nona Tucker*
J. Carrol Naish *as Henry Devers*
Beulah Bondi *as Grandma*
Percy Kilbride *as Harmie Jenkins*
Blanche Yurka *as Mom*
Charles Kemper *as Tim*
Norman Lloyd *as Finley Hewitt*
Estelle Taylor *as Lizzie*
Noreen Nash *as Becky*
Jack Norworth *as the doctor*
Paul Harvey *as Ruston*
Jay Gilpin *as Jot*
Jean Vanderbilt *as Daisy*
Nestor Piva *as the bartender*
Paul Burns *as Uncle Pete*
Dorothy Granger *as a girl at the dance*

Earl Hodgkins *as a wedding guest*
Almira Sessions *as a customer in the store*
Rex *as Zoonie*
Florence Bates *as Rose*

THE DIARY OF A CHAMBERMAID, made in 1946.
86 minutes

Directed by Jean Renoir
Screenplay adapted by Jean Renoir and Burgess Meredith
     from the novel by Octave Mirbeau and the play by
     André Leuse, André de Lorde, and Thielly Nores
Produced by Benedict Bogeaus, Burgess Meredith
Photographed by Lucien Andriot
Assistant director Joseph Landew
Edited by James Smith
Music by Michel Michelet
Sets by Eugène Lourié
Costumes by Barbara Karinska

CAST:

Paulette Godard *as Célestine*
Burgess Meredith *as Captain Mauger*
Francis Lederer *as Joseph*
Hurd Hatfield *as Georges*
Reginald Owen *as Lanlaire*
Judith Anderson *as Mrs. Lanlaire*
Irene Ryan *as Louise*
Florence Bates *as Rose*
Almira Sessions *as Marianne*

THE WOMAN ON THE BEACH, made in 1946.
71 minutes

Directed by Jean Renoir
Screenplay by Jean Renoir, Frank Davis, J. R. Michael
    Hogan, adapted from the Mitchell Wilson novel *None
    So Blind*
Produced by Jack Gross and Will Price
Photographed by Harry Wild and Leo Tover
Assistant director James Casey
Edited by Ronald Gross
Music by Hanns Eisler
Sets by Darrell Silvera

CAST:

Joan Bennett *as Peggy Butler*
Robert Ryan *as Lieutenant Scott Burnett*
Charles Bickford *as Ted Butler*
Nan Leslie *as Eve Geddes*
Walter Sande *as Otto Wernecke*
Irene Ryan *as Mrs. Wernecke*
Frank Darien *as Lars*
Jay Norris *as Jimmy*
Glenn Vernon *as Kirk*

THE RIVER, made in 1949-50 (Technicolor).
99 minutes

Directed by Jean Renoir
Screenplay by Rumer Godden and Jean Renoir from the
    Rumer Godden novel
Produced by Kenneth McEldowney, Kalyan Gupta, and
    Jean Renoir

Photographed by Claude Renoir and Ramananda Sen
    Gupta
Assistant directors J. Das Gupta, Sukhano y Sen, and Bansi
    Ashe
Edited by George Gale
Music by M. A. Partha Sarathy
Sets by Bansi Chandra Gupta

CAST:

Nora Swinburne *as the mother*
Esmond Knight *as the father*
Patricia Walters *as Harriet*
Radha *as Melanie*
Adrienne Corri *as Valerie*
Thomas E. Breen *as Captain John*
Arthur Shields *as Mr. John*
Richard Foster *as Bogey*
Suprova Mukerjee *as Nan*
Penelope Wilkinson *as Elizabeth*
Jane Harris *as Muffie*
Sahjan Singh *as Ram Prasad Singh*
Nimai Barik *as Kanu*
Trilak Jetley *as Anil*
June Hillman *as the narrator*
Jennifer Harris *as Mouse*
Cecilia Wood *as Victoria*

LE CARROSSE D'OR, made in 1953 (Technicolor).
100 minutes

Directed by Jean Renoir
Screenplay by Jean Renoir, Jack Kirkland, Renzo Avanzo,

Giulio Macchi, and Ginette Doynel; adapted from the
Prosper Mérimée play *Le Carrosse du Saint-Sacrement*
Produced by Francesco Alliata
Photographed by Claude Renoir
Assistant directors Marc Maurette and Giulio Macchi
Edited by Mario Serandrei and David Hawkins
Music by Vivaldi; adapted by Gino Marinozzi
Sets by Mario Chiari assisted by Gianni Poldori
Costumes by Mario de Matteis

CAST:

Anna Magnani *as Camilla*
Duncan Lamont *as the Viceroy*
Odoardo Spadaro *as Don Antonio*
Ricardo Rioli *as Ramon*
Paul Campbell *as Felipe*
Nada Fiorelli *as Isabelle*
George Higgins *as Martinez*
Dante *as Arlequin*
Rino *as the doctor*
Gisella Matthews *as Marquise Altamirano*
Ralph Truman *as the Duke of Castro*
Elena Altieri *as the Duchess of Castro*
Renato Chiantoni *as Captain Fracesse*
Giulio Tedeschi *as Baldassare*
Alfredo Kolner *as Florindo*
Alfredo Medini *as Ploichinelle*
Medini Brothers *as the four child acrobats*
John Pasetti *as the Captain of the Guards*
William Tubbs *as the innkeeper*
Cecil Matthews *as the Baron*
Fedo Keeling *as the Viscount*

Jean Debucourt *as the Bishop*
Lina Marengo *as the old comedienne*
Raf de la Terre *as the magistrate*

FRENCH CANCAN, made in 1954 (Technicolor).
97 minutes

Directed by Jean Renoir
Screenplay by Jean Renoir from an idea by André-Paul
     Antoine
Produced by Louis Wipf
Photographed by Michel Kelber with Henri Tiquet
Assistant directors Serge Vallin, Pierre Kast, and Jacques
     Rivette
Choreography by G. Grandgean
Edited by Boris Lewin
Music by Georges Van Parys and an assortment of tunes
     from the cafés-concert of the turn of the century; lyrics
     by Jean Renoir
Sets by Max Douy
Costumes by Rosine Delamare

CAST:

Jean Gabin *as Danglard*
Françoise Arnoul *as Nini*
Maria Félix *as the Abbess*
Jean-Roger Caussimon *as Baron Walter*
Max Dalban *as the owner of "Reine Blanche"*
Dora Doll *as La Génisse*
Gaston Modot *as Danglard's servant*

Gianni Esposito *as Prince Alexandre*
Valentine Tessier *as Mme. Olympe*
Michèle Philippe *as Eléonore*
Jean Parédès *as Coudrier*
Lydia Johnson *as Guibole*
Anna Amendola *as Esther Georges*
Philippe Clay *as Casimir*
France Roche *as Béatrix*
Annik Morice *as Thérèse*
Jacques Jouanneau *as Bidon*
Michèle Nadal *as Bigoudi*
Sylvine Delannoy *as Titine*
Anne-Marie Merson *as Paquita*
Albert Rémy *as Barjolin*
Michel Piccoli *as Valorgueil*
Patachou *as Yvette Guilbert*
André Claveau *as Paul Delmet*
Edith Piaf *as Eugénie Buffet*
Jean Raymond *as Paulus*
Jean-Marc Tennberg *as Savatte*
Pierre Olaf *as the heckler*
Leo Campion *as the Commandant*
Jacque Catelain *as the minister*
Hubert Beauchamps *as Isidore*
Mme. Pacquerette *as Mimi Prunelle*
Gaston Gabarouche *as Oscar, the pianist*
Pierre Moncorbier *as the bailiff*
Jean Mortier *as the hotel manager*
Robert Auboyneau *as the elevator operator*
Laurence Bataille *as the pygmy*
Jacques Ciron ⎫
Claude Arnay ⎭ *dandies*

Chauffard *as the police inspector*
Jacques Hilling *as the surgeon*
Jedlinska *as la gigolette*
Jean Sylvère *as the groom*
Palmyre Levasseur *as a laundress*

ELÉNA ET LES HOMMES, made in 1956 (English-
    language title *PARIS DOES STRANGE THINGS*)
    (Eastman-color).

95 minutes

Directed by Jean Renoir
Screenplay by Jean Renoir with Jean Serge
Produced by Louis Wipf
Photographed by Claude Renoir
Assistant director Serge Vallin
Edited by Boris Lewin
Music by Joseph Kosma; songs by Juliette Greco and Leo
    Marjane, with other songs of the period
Sets by Jean André
Costumes by Rosine Delamare and Monique Plotin

CAST:

Ingrid Bergman *as Eléna*
Jean Marais *as General Rollan*
Mel Ferrer *as Henri de Chevincourt*
Jean Richard *as Hector, Rollan's servant*
Magali Noël *as Lolotte, Eléna's maid*
Juliette Greco *as Miarka*
Pierre Bertin *as Martin Michaud*

Jacques Jouanneau *as Eugène Godin*
Jacques Morel *as Duchêne*
Jean Claudio *as Lionel*
Renaud Mary *as Fleury*
Elina Labourdette *as Paulette*
Jean Castanier *as Isnard*
Mirko Ellis *as Marbeau*
Gaston Modot *as Romani, the leader of the gypsies*
Gregori Chmara *as Eléna's servant*
Paul Demange *as a spectator*
Jim Gerald *as a cafe owner*
Dora Doll *as Rosa la Rose*
Leó Marjane *as the street singer*
Michèle Nadal *as Denise Gaudin*
Claire Gérard *as a woman in the street*
Robert LeBéal *as the doctor*
Albert Remy *as Buchez*
Olga Valéry *as Olga*
Frédérik Duvallès *as Godin*

L'ALBUM DE FAMILLE DE JEAN RENOIR, made in
      1956.
27 minutes

Directed by Roland Gritti
Screenplay by Pierre Desgraupes
Produced for Paris Télévision
Photographed by Jean Tournier

CAST:

Jean Renoir
Pierre Desgraupes

LE TESTAMENT DU DOCTEUR CORDELIER, made in
   1959 (English title *EXPERIMENT IN EVIL*).
95 minutes

Directed by Jean Renoir
Screenplay by Jean Renoir; freely adapted from Robert
   Louis Stevenson's *Dr. Jekyll and Mr. Hyde*
Produced by Albert Hollebecke, and Cie Jean Renoir
Photographed by Georges Leclerc
Assistant director Maurice Beuchey
Edited by Renée Lichtig
Music by Joseph Kosma
Sets by Marcel-Louis Dieulot
Costumes by Monique Durand

CAST:

Jean-Louis Barrault *as Dr. Cordelier and Opale*
Michel Vitold *as Dr. Séverin*
Teddy Bilis *as Joly*
Micheline Gary *as Marguérite*
Jean Topart *as Désiré*
Gaston Modot *as the gardener, Blaise*
Jacque Catelain *as the ambassador*
Régine Blaess *as his wife*
Jacqueline Morane *as Alberte*
André Certes *as Inspector Salabris*
Jacques Dannoville *as Commissaire Lardout*
Jean Renoir *as the narrator*
Jean-Pierre Granval *as the hotel manager*
Jean Bertho *as a passerby*
Didier d'Yd *as Georges*
Raymond Jourdan *as the cripple*
Raymone *as Mme. des Essarts*

Madeleine Marion *as Juliette*
Primerose Perret *as Mary*
Sylviane Margolle *as the little girl*
Dominique Dangan *as the mother*
Ghislaine Dumont *as Suzy*
Claudie Bourlon *as Lise*
Jacqueline Frot *as Isabelle*
Françoise Boyer *as Françoise*
Annick Allières *as a neighbor*

LE DÉJEUNER SUR L'HERBE, made in 1959 (Eastman-
color).
92 minutes

Directed by Jean Renoir
Screenplay by Jean Renoir
Produced by Ginette Courtois-Doynel
Photographed by Georges Leclerc
Assistant directors Maurice Beuchey, Francis Morane,
    Jean-Pierre Spicro, Hedy Naka, and Jean de Nesles
Edited by Renée Lichtig under the direction of Maurice
    Beuchey
Music by Joseph Kosma
Sets by Marcel-Louis Dieulot
Costumes by Monique Dunan

CAST:

Paul Meurisse *as Étienne Alexis*
Catérine Rouvel *as Nénette*
Jacqueline Morane *as Titine, her eldest sister*

Fernand Sardou *as Nino, Étienne's father*
Jean-Pierre Granval *as Titine's husband*
Robert Chandeau *as Laurent*
Micheline Gary *as Madeline, his wife*
Frédéric O'Brady *as Rudolf*
Ingrid Nordine *as Marie-Charlotte*
Charles Blavette *as Gaspard, the shepherd*
Jean Claudio *as Rousseau, the steward*
Ghislaine Dumont *as Magda, Rudolf's wife*
Hélène Duc *as Isabelle*
Jacques Dannoville *as M. Paignant*
Marguerite Cassan *as his wife*
Raymond Jourdan *as Eustache, the cook*
François Miege *as Barthélmy, the chauffeur*
Régine Blaess *as Claire, the maid*
Pierre Leproux *as Bailly*
Michel Herbault *as Montet*
Jacqueline Fontel *as Miss Michelet, the secretary*
Paulette Dubost *as Miss Forestier, the telephonist*
Andre Brunot *as the curé*
M. You *as the foreman, Chapuis*
Dupraz, Lucas, Thierry, and Péricart *as announcers*

LE CAPORAL ÉPINGLÉ, made in 1961-62 (English title
        THE VANISHING CORPORAL; American title
        THE ELUSIVE CORPORAL).

105 minutes

Directed by Jean Renoir
Screenplay by Jean Renoir and Guy Lefranc from a Jacques
        Perret novel

Produced by Réne G. Vuattuox
Photographed by Georges Leclerc
Codirector Guy Lefranc
Assistant director Marc Maurette
Edited by Renée Lichtig assisted by Madeleine Lacompère
Music by Joseph Kosma
Sets by Eugène Herrly

CAST:

Jean-Pierre Cassel *as the Corporal*
Claude Brasseur *as Pater*
Claude Rich *as Ballochet*
Jean Carmet *as Émile*
Jacques Jouanneau *as Penchagauche*
Mario David *as Caruso*
O. E. Hasse *as the drunk on the train*
Philippe Castelli *as the electrician*
Guy Bédos *as the stutterer*
Raymond Jourdan *as Dupieu*
Gérard Darrieu *as the squinter*
Sacha Briquet *as the prisoner escaping dressed as a woman*
François Darbon *as the French soldier married to a German woman*
Lucien Raimbourg *as the station guard*

LA DIRECTION D'ACTEUR PAR JEAN RENOIR, made in 1968.

27 minutes

Directed by Jean Renoir
Produced by Roger Fleytoux

Photographed by Edmond Richard
Edited by Mireille Mauberna

CAST:

Jean Renoir
Gisèle Braunberger } *as themselves*

THE CHRISTIAN LIQUORICE STORE, made in 1969.

90 minutes

Directed by James Frawley

Jean Renoir *as himself*

LE PETIT THÉÂTRE DE JEAN RENOIR, made in 1969.

100 minutes

Directed by Jean Renoir
Screenplay by Jean Renoir
Produced by Pierre Long and Jean Renoir for television
Photographed by Georges Leclerc
Assistant director Denis Epstein
Edited by Geneviève Winding, assisted by Gisèle Chezeau
Music for "Le Dernier Reveillon" by Jean Weiner
   for "La Cireuse Électrique" by Joseph Kosma
   for "La Belle Époque" song by Octave Crémieux
    and G. Millandy
   for "Le Roi d'Yvetôt" by Jean Weiner
Sets by Gilbert Margerie

CAST:

Introductions by Jean Renoir

"Le Dernier Reveillon" (*"The Last Christmas Eve"*)
Nino Formicola *as le Clochard*
Milly Monti *as la Clocharde*
Roland Bertin *as Gontran*
André Dumas *as the manager*
Robert Lombard *as the maître d'hôtel*
Roger Trapp *as Max Vialle*

"La Cireuse Électrique" (*"The Electric Waxing Machine"*)
Marguerite Cassan *as Émilie*
Pierre Olaf *as Gustave*
Jacques Dynam *as Jules*
Jean-Louis Tristan *as electric waxing machine salesman*
Denis Gunzburg ⎫
Claude Guillame ⎭ *the lovers*

"La Belle Époque"
Jeanne Moreau *as the singer*

"Le Roi d'Yvetôt" (*"The King of Yvetot"*)
Fernand Sardou *as Duvallier, Roi d'Yvetôt*
Françoise Arnoul *as Isabelle, his wife*
Jean Carmet *as Ferand*
Andrex *as M. Blanc*
Roger Prégor *as Maître Joly*
Edmond Ardisson *as César*
Dominique Labourier *as Paulette*

AND

1954 Debut as a theater director, when he staged a Grisha and Mitsou Dabet adaptation of William Shakespeare's *Julius Caesar*

CAST:

Henri Vidal *as Julius Caesar*
Jean-Pierre Aumont *as Mark Anthony*
Loleh Bellon *as Portia*
Yves Robert *as Cassius*
Françoise Christophe *as Calpurnia*
Paul Meurisse *as Brutus*
Jean Parédès *as Casca*
Jean Topart *as Octavius Caesar*
And others

1955 Second theater direction when Jean Renoir staged
          Orvet, a comedy in three acts written by him for
          Leslie Caron in 1953
Music by Joseph Kosma
Sets by Georges Wakhevitch
Costumes by Karinska and Givenchy

CAST:

Leslie Caron *as Orvet*
Paul Meurisse *as Georges*
Michel Herbault *as Olivier*
Catherine Le Couey *as Mme. Camus*
Raymond Bussières *as Coutant*
Jacques Jouanneau *as William*
Marguerite Cassan *as Clotilde*
Yorick Royan *as Berthe*
Suzanne Courtal *as Mother Viper*
Pierre Olaf *as Philippe*
Georges Saillard *as the doctor*
Georges Hubert ⎫ *huntsmen*
Henry Charrett ⎭

1956 Renoir wrote a play, *Carola,* and adapted Clifford
Odets' play *The Big Knife*

1957 Renoir wrote the story for a short ballet on the war,
"Le Feu aux Poudres," which was performed by
Ludmilla Tcherina as the first part of a dance
program named "Les Amants de Teruel"

1958 Renoir wrote a biographical study of Auguste
Renoir titled *Renoir, My Father*

1968 Renoir wrote a novel called *Les Cahiers du Capitaine
Georges*

1974 Renoir wrote *My Life and My Films*

Index

(Italicized numbers indicate listing in filmography)